Charonia
tritonis

Mitra
mitra

Fusinus
colus

Melo
amphorus

Vasum
turbinellus

Epitonium
scalare

Hippopus
hippopus

Cardium
costatum

Pitar
dione

She Sells
SEASHELLS

SHE SELLS

SEASHELLS

Veronica Parker Johns

FUNK & WAGNALLS
New York

She Sells

SEASHELLS

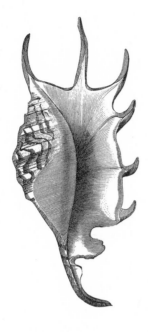

One

Yes, I sell seashells, but they were not always my stock in trade as well as my chief delight. I was a grown girl, past forty-five and considered quite bright for my age, when they entered my life. It was a case of love at first sight.

Of course I'd seen shells before, but none of any particular distinction. Suddenly seeing them at their best was like being introduced to filet mignon after a lifelong diet of mush. I became positively ravenous; to this day I have not had enough.

To paraphrase Auntie Mame, whose language was somewhat more pungent, "Life is a banquet, yet a lot of poor souls are starving to death." So it is with shells, which can provide a spiritual feast fit for a king if one is but aware of them.

SHE SELLS SEASHELLS

Once shells were exclusively the property of kings and princes; no one below the rank of earl could aspire to a noteworthy collection. This was in the golden age of exploration, when sailing vessels prowled the earth in search of new wonders with which to astound the folks back home. Among the most prized and high-priced novelties were shells unlike any ever seen in Europe.

Almost every well-appointed castle had its shell cabinet. Scholars of the natural sciences were constantly visiting in one or another of them for as long as it took to sort, identify, and catalogue the specimens. It was big business in that small world, but strictly for the carriage trade.

Now, although every man is king and there are two carriages in every garage, relatively few people have seashells they can call their own. The worst of it is that they don't know what they are missing, just as I did not realize my lack until that lucky day when things took a turn for the better.

During the preceding, wasted years, I had gone where the shells were and overlooked them. I had taken a round-the-world cruise, visited Florida, the West Indies, Mexico, and our own West Coast, and had never seen a shell. I had waded into the Indian Ocean, the Caribbean Sea, and the Gulfs of Mexico and California, but had not taken the trouble to stoop over to find out what was beneath my feet, because nobody had told me it might be interesting.

I was, like almost everyone else, a victim of what I suspect is a conspiracy. It is hard not to be melodramatic about this because I believe that a conspiracy of silence, fostered by a vast inertia and almost willful ignorance, has kept people from seashells and seashells from people. The Philistines who thrive on the commonplace have managed to reduce the complicated science of conchology to the level of a problem that can be solved by little minds during one sunny afternoon on the beach.

There is no durable thing in nature with more infinite variety than seashells. There are over one hundred thousand recognized species (only the insect kingdom exceeds this total) and, within each species, each specimen is as nonconforming as a snowflake. Yet, if one out of ten persons says seashells to the other nine, the mental responses conjured up will be of shards found on beaches, a tinted horror with "Welcome to Miami" inscribed upon it, or a pin tray encrusted with itsy-bitsy dyed shells that keep coming unglued. Of these latter two types of indignities to shells the less said the better. They have done the most to give shells a bad name.

There is a dirty word applied to shells, for which we should hang our heads in shame. "Dust-catchers," some persons call them, which is absolutely ridiculous. It is not in the nature of shells to catch dust since their natural habitat is notoriously free of that substance. If there is dust in the air for shells to catch, it is our fault, not theirs. Apology rather than opprobrium is due, even as it is long past overdue to those natives who caught measles and other scourges of civilization from seafaring strangers. Since we are to blame if our shells grow dingy, is it too much trouble to wash them now and again, considering the joy they give?

Shells acquired the label of "dust catchers" in the Victorian parlors where they were only part of the unmanageable, undustable clutter. This cliché, and others, have persisted because there has never been an organized counteroffensive of truth. Such an offensive would suffer from a shortage of troops for I daresay that more otherwise well-informed people know less about seashells than any other subject. They don't even suspect how much they do not know. One does not have to be a botanist to be aware that there are differing and marvelous plants all over the world. One has not seen, nor will one ever see all of them, yet one has enough working knowledge of their specifications to be able to imagine what they are like. One almost has to be a conchologist, however, to imagine the infinite variety of seashells.

A person who has only seen what the waves toss up on beaches or shells tortured into a tawdry brooch cannot possibly visualize what others are like. It is demanding too much of the human mind to expect it to compute with such meager data. One might as well ask a machine programmed only in Urdu to reel off the sonnets of Shakespeare.

Most first-time visitors to my seashell shop are confounded and ask such questions as "How long has this been going on?" and "Why didn't I know?" Surprisingly many of them have asked, "How can people see these things and not believe in God?"

Dead specimens found on the beach, however pretty, do not begin to tell the story. For its beauty to endure, a shell must be collected while the mollusk that constructed it is still alive. Thus, as with many things having to do with beauty, at the primary level of shell collecting there are overtones of cruelty and the predatory nature of man.

Has unwillingness to bear this guilt been a factor in the suppression of seashells? I doubt it. We humans are not all that humane or we would never wear fur and feathers nor eat oysters when they "R in season." Incidentally, even the most gorgeous shells are housing for somebody's seafood dinner, so their harvesting can be considered justifiable on that basis alone. However, right this minute on an island in the Indian Ocean a man may be throwing away a shell worth three thousand dollars while his wife makes mollusk stew of the meat. It is ignorance, not tender-heartedness, that keeps shells from people.

The very word we English-speakers chose to describe shells is part of the conspiracy and has created a semantic impasse. A shell is also that part of an egg or a peanut or a clam that you discard. Don't eat it! It's bad for you. Spit it out in Mommy's hand, it's nasty.

Shells that are seen can overcome this handicap, but what about shells not seen, or seen only with the debris of the sea still upon them, before they have been carefully cleaned to show their loveliness? I weep for those millions of shells tossed away daily because their beauty and worth were unknown. How can one reach each inhabitant of Oceania to tell him that attention must be paid? One cannot, of course, but one can make a start in that direction from the top, hoping that the news will trickle down and stay that man's arm with the intimation that he might get something for the nothing he is throwing away.

One of the most enjoyable emotions we shell lovers experience as we gloat over our treasures is a sense of triumph that these things have been snatched from destruction; that they have miraculously come from so far out, so deep down, to a haven where they are appreciated. Had the mollusk not been taken by force from the sea it would, in due course, have died; no one would have known it had lived, but here in our hands is evidence of its existence that will live on forever. In a world of ephemeras, this means a lot.

But from what source can the news start trickling? Bigger

and better displays in museums would seem to be the answer. Attendance at museums is not compulsory, but hordes of people do go to them. An attractive exhibit of shells might send some individuals to libraries (where, parenthetically and unfortunately, they will find few books on the subject) to learn more. Key people, like school teachers, might be inspired to explore this new old frontier with their classes.

However, the sorry truth of the matter is that museums, with few exceptions, are active participants in the conspiracy against seashells.

School children are guided through natural history museums so they may learn to appreciate the marvels of nature. They see beady-eyed stuffed animals in well-staged habitat groups. They see artifacts of cave dwellers and skeletons of prehistoric mammals. They learn about the origins of coal and oil. They see minerals, precious gems, birds, tree trunks, bugs, snakes, and what-have-you. One of them, with a little bit of luck, may get lost on his way back from the washroom and stumble upon two or three badly-lit cases containing a mess of seashells. Yet upstairs in the museum, where research is done, there may be thousands of shell specimens, both rare and common, available for viewing to the bona fide student, by appointment only.

I am constantly having to defend the shell department of New York City's American Museum of Natural History against my customers' complaints. It is not the department's fault that only five cases of shells are now on display, or that until recently there had not been a single shell in sight for years.

Once there was a great Hall of Oceanography with hundreds of shells sharing ample space with other sea creatures;

then the conspirators took over. The hall was closed for repairs. It remained closed, and little bits of it were nibbled away for use by other departments. Even though the museum grew and grew there was less and less space for shells. Several generations grew up without being introduced to them.

Instead of being accused of stinginess for sharing so few of its goodies with the public, the department should be praised for having at least acquired those five cases. There is no separate department of mollusks at the American Museum but merely a small band of enthusiasts working within the Department of Living Invertebrates consisting of a couple of professionals assisted by the efforts and bequests of amateurs. Much of the cataloguing is done by volunteers or by workers whose pay comes from the gifts of amateurs. A bequest from a shell lover financed those aforesaid five cases. A donation from the New York Shell Club, an organization of zealots, provided a display of shells indigenous to this area.

Although the problem of the local museum is nearest to my heart, it is one that is by no means unique. The position of the Smithsonian Institution is not much better. The British Museum, which owns an example of every species found by the early conchologists, houses its collection in a musty old building out by the Albert Memorial. One must have absolutely smashing credentials to be permitted to see it, not to mention a superb sense of direction to be able to find it.

Like icebergs, most museum collections are nine-tenths invisible. Why? Because their curators are low men on the budgetary totem poles, barely able to make ends meet. Space can always be found for another group of gnus and elands because wealthy patrons like to go on tax deductible safaris. People of means, like the rest of us, enjoy digging in ancient middens, so the anthropological department never needs to pass the hat.

There are too few people eager to disseminate the story of seashells because they have never heard it themselves. The conspirators have arranged to infiltrate every museum board in the world with someone who has been exposed only to the shards on the beach and the pin trays and is consequently certain that no one could possibly be interested in shells. So the vicious circle narrows. If I sound bitter, I am.

Meanwhile, the secret is leaking out. The underground of the undersea world is functioning better than ever. People are traveling more. Diving equipment is both more reliable and reasonable. The glass-bottomed boat has even starred in a movie that played Radio City Music Hall.

And I have this little outpost on Third Avenue where I do my missionary work against the forces of darkness. Everyone with a head for business tells me that I cannot possibly make enough money selling seashells to justify a high rental in busy midtown Manhattan; that I should seek a storefront on a side street, or stick with tradition and sell them by the seashore. As if I didn't know! What *they* don't understand is that I, like all missionaries, have things beyond money on my mind.

I want maximum exposure for my wares. For far too long have shells been relegated to side streets and the shores. I want mine to be on a busy avenue; the more crowded with passers-by the better. Actually, what it is is a people-trap, baited with specimens so provocative that I have been able to catch hundreds. Some of them wriggle and squirm, not being suffi-ciently in a state of grace to get the message immediately, but a gratifyingly large number respond at once, telling me I have opened a whole new world to them. When they can tear themselves away, they leave to spread the tidings.

Hallelujah!

Even when the shop is closed, the good work goes on. At all hours of the night, people pause and stare at the lovely things in the window, murmuring, "That's a seashell? How long has this been going on?" How long? For ages, folks; seashells were here before we were. Maybe that's what some people cannot abide.

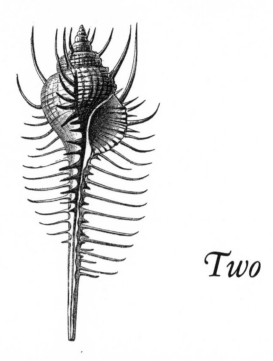

Two

"How did you get into this?" many people ask me.

I get a "cauld grue" every time I think of how nearly I did not, of the elaborate net Fate had to weave to enmesh me. It was a case of pure serendipity. I was looking for something else, and I found seashells.

It was the autumn of 1954. I was a writer of mysteries, at the time between plots, not knowing where my next one was coming from, and thinking it might be a good idea to try another tack. Memoirs of one's quaint, cantankerous relatives were much in fashion just then, but regrettably none of my relatives about whom I had anything like total recall was especially interesting. Then an item in the *Herald Tribune* caught my eye. The headline read, "SHELL-DEALER HERE PAYS $1000.00 FOR SHELL." I was interested, though skeptical. Who would pay that much money for someone's trash, however pretty it might be? This was obviously the dream of some press agent; I wondered why he had been inactive a few months earlier when I was combing the town for offbeat shops to list in a guidebook on which I was collaborating. A seashell shop, for goodness' sake! What next? As we say in mysteries, "had I but known."

I read on to make the startling discovery that the proprietor of this odd enterprise was my first cousin once removed, Crosbie McArthur, whom I had not seen nor communicated with since I was six years old when my family visited his in Ohio. Except for that fact, I would have filed and forgotten the clipping until such time as the guidebook required revision. I would not have been inspired to go out of my way to see mere shells, whatever the value assigned to them. As it was, I went as soon as I could fetch my hat and coat, the finger of Fate having beckoned with her customary duplicity.

McArthur's mother, my great-aunt Jane, was a genuine character, meriting a full-length biography if a doting son could supply the details. A jolly French-Canadian girl, Jane was the youngest of three sisters whose drive to succeed had always fascinated me. Of a nationality in which, at that time, the male was dominant and usually kept his woman in the kitchen, barefoot, and in an age in which women were not expected to do much of anything, the sisters had carved out careers for themselves and gone about as far as they could go. Given today's more favorable climate, who knows what heights they might have scaled, starting from that humble hamlet outside Montreal where they were born?

Eliza, the eldest, became the Mother General of an order of nuns, filling the top command post with awesome efficiency. I knew, however, that a book about her could never become a best seller outside ecclesiastical circles; it would have absolutely no love interest, nor the required spice of conflict. After all, she had not had to wrestle with male competition for her job.

Then there was the middle girl, Agnes, my grandmother. She became one of the leading Christian Science practitioners in New York City in the early 1900s. She had some male competition, I suppose, but not of the to-the-death sort. She also had the drawback, from a biographer's point of view, of having married a man who simultaneously made a success in his own field, who not only placed no roadblocks in her way but saw to it that such obstacles were removed, and quickly. Whence would come the tug at the heartstrings?

Jane was more like it. I knew only the barest facts about her because members of my family lack that wholesome—or snoopy—interest in each other's comings and goings. Perhaps we are too reticent, or each individual is too self-centered. I had one elderly relation, Cousin Evie, who knew whom everybody married and what was worn at the weddings, but she was such a bore that I did not listen to her. She was from the other side of the family, though, and knew nothing of Jane.

What I knew was that Jane McArthur, with an ailing husband and four small bairns to care for, had rocketed around Ohio at the turn of the century in a buckboard, selling real estate in what was later to become downtown Cleveland. There, in one sentence, is her biography. I mean all of it, because McArthur also proved to be a victim of the family curse of reticence. Doting son he was, yet he added no flesh to the bones, and that's why Greer Garson never made a movie of Jane's life.

I set out with high hopes and a clutch of snapshots of six-year-old me and his teen-age brother to establish my identity and open the gates of memory. I did not take the pictures out of my handbag that day, because the moment I saw the shells I forgot everything else.

The shop was then on East Sixty-first Street, a hole-in-the-wall measuring nine-by-nine, and it was exploding with seashells of all shapes, all sizes, all colors. It was like being in the middle of the fountains and fireworks finale at the New York World's Fair. I wanted to see all of the shells at once, and yet not take my eyes from one to look at another.

What excited me most was the strength of the things. "Dainty" is so often paired with "seashell" that I had thought it an inevitable coupling. Instantly, several substitute words came to mind: "dramatic," "disturbing," "flamboyant." To this day I am anti-dainty, which does not mean that I do not appreciate the delicacy of a tiny specimen, but what wins me is that despite its apparent daintiness, it had to be tough as a stevedore to win out over overwhelming odds. Dainty shells would long since have pounded themselves into extinction on the world's beaches, leaving only fossilized reminders.

These indomitable beauties had survived the tumult, found their niches, and clung to them, evolved in their separate ways into more different species than anything in nature except insects. Each was a bit of nature that one could own and keep. I wanted to own them all. It was the prodigal profusion that got me and still holds me enthralled; the never-endingness, the expectation that a shell more gorgeous than any you have ever

[13]

seen is just about to appear. I felt I could not possibly live long enough to see as many as I wanted to see, but vowed to keep looking as long as I lived.

I also felt a sense of urgency, a need to make up for lost time. I was furious at all who had downgraded these marvels by calling them "dainty" and making meretricious curios of them. Robert Louis Stevenson said of mollusks that they were the only creatures who build their own monuments in their lifetimes; in a Pantheon of monuments, I was very nearly moved to tears.

It isn't all tears and reverence, of course. After one gets over that initial shock one can get quite chummy with shells, able to talk out loud in their presence, instead of whispering as so many of my customers do, giving me the eerie feeling that I, like my great-aunt Eliza and grandmother Agnes, am something of a *réligieuse*. I don't feel that way at all. It is more of a simple primitive faith in which you take wonders as daily bread, although you never take them for granted, and can sing and dance to celebrate them instead of beating your breast.

Nevertheless there still come moments, say when I am opening a parcel from the Philippines and unwrap a shell so special, so poignantly beautiful or so touchingly funny that it brings tears to my eyes and I thank Heaven for the privilege of seeing it. Then I am again the novice of that day on Sixty-first Street, awestruck and very, very humble.

Fate had concealed more than one trick up her sleeve that day; simultaneously involving me with seashells while solving a problem for Cousin Crosbie. To accomplish this double-play she had to introduce a third *dramatis persona* to play a bit part often enacted in the shop—that of the "Girl Who Cannot Make Up Her Mind."

SHE SELLS SEASHELLS

Torn between the interior pinkness of one *Murex erythrostomus,* and the superior size of another, she decided to postpone the critical choice until a future date.

"I'll come in when I have more time," she said. "You're open on Saturdays, aren't you?"

"We usually are," said McArthur, "but for the next two months we won't be."

Panicking, the girl bought both shells—a shopper after my own heart, since that is how I always solve such dilemmas. Then, clutching her paper sack, she went off to worry about lunch money, having put first things first.

"Why won't the shop be open on Saturdays?" I asked my cousin indignantly, wondering how he could be so cruel as to deny a poor addict a nonworking day in which to indulge herself at leisure.

His excuse, feeble it seemed to me, was that he was going abroad. His assistant, a devout Orthodox Jew, would not tend store on the Sabbath. The die was cast. Veronica Parker Johns rode to the rescue to keep all the shell-happy people happy. It was the humane thing to do and, besides, think of all the shells I would get to see and sit around with.

The detail I overlooked was that I knew absolutely nothing about seashells—and that the subject was a whale of a big one.

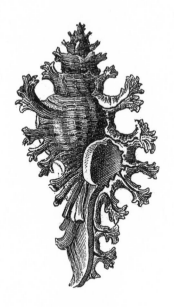

Three

Crosbie McArthur did not fret about details either. A genie had materialized me in the nick of time. This was Friday; he was sailing the following morning. He had long since resigned himself to missing the Saturday trade when, out of the blue, popped I, a blood relative and therefore constrained not to rob him blind.

I know now that he made it all sound a little too easy. The hardest thing, it appeared, would be to open the door. The key sometimes stuck, but if I had any trouble I should ask the Chinaman in the laundry next door who had had plenty of experience with the problem. The rest would be a breeze, he implied. Every shell was tagged with its Latin name and price.

I could read, couldn't I? In my free moments I could look at the pretty pictures in the reference books we had for sale and become an expert over the weekend.

Now, more than twelve years later, I am still not an expert nor do I ever expect to be. Super experts can still make me feel as stupid as I did on my debut that Saturday when, as luck would have it, waiting at the door while I fiddled with the key and then ran for the Chinaman was one of the great ladies of shell collecting, whom I have since grown to know and love. That day, she terrified me.

When we were finally inside and I had found the proper light switch after two mistakes, she asked me if I had a blue *Patella*. A blue *Patella*, for Pete's sake! A patella, I knew, was a kneecap. I had two of them. They were knocking together.

Actually, Mrs. Crain was being most kind, phrasing the question in what was almost baby talk for a scientific collector. If she had not guessed that I was very, very green, she would have come out flat-footed and asked for a *Nomaeopelta meso-leuca,* and thrown me into an even deeper depression.

I use Latin names now, following my own rules as to pronunciation, not as an affectation but simply because there are not enough apt common names to cover all the shells. Some people think that what has kept the world of conchology small is its smug insistence upon Latin nomenclature; I intend to prove otherwise.

First, I will address myself to those who know as little as I did on that historic Saturday in 1954. The more advanced students may leave the room if they wish but, please, no loud roughhousing in the corridors. The rest of us are trying to learn.

What is so difficult about the kindergarten class of conchology is that for the most basic questions there are no answers. Much must be taken on faith. There has not been enough research done (thanks to our arch enemies, the conspirators) to resolve all the "Hows?"; and for most of the "Whys?" the best replies are "Why nots?"

At first, defensive about my own limitations, when people asked, "What is this?" I jumped way ahead of them. Assuming that everyone was leagues ahead of *me,* I thought they meant, "Which cone is this?" or "Which murex?" To throw them off the scent I would frown and say, "It will come to me in a minute. It isn't *Conus litteratus."* Or, "It isn't *Murex erythrostomus,"* those being the first two names I had mastered. Likely as not the potential customer would say, "Oh?", look at me peculiarly, and leave the shop, never to return. How to lose friends for shells and alienate customers. Now I know better.

As I have said before and will doubtless say again, shells excite some people and make them ask silly questions, to which they deserve wholly serious answers in language they are equipped to understand. The trick is to tune in on their respective wavelengths to determine just how far back to begin. There are some individuals, at the lowest level, whose "What is this?," uttered irritably, can be freely translated as "Is it an ashtray? Is it a soap dish? If it isn't something sensible why are you wasting my time selling it in a store?" They get the squelch direct, the haughty, "Why, it's *Conus litteratus,* of course. Any three-year-old child could identify it." This method is also used for the genus Jackanapes, the type who probably laughs uproariously at sad foreign movies he cannot understand. He brings in his cronies to look at "the nutty lady who runs a shop selling nuttin' but shells." The nutty lady snaps into her czarina mood, straightens her tiara, and lets him have it, improvising freely:

"A good question. Linné once called it *Conus cedonulli,* but some authorities believe it was actually the same shell he called *Conus ammiralis.* Or, on the contrary, *cedonulli* might be Gmelin's *Conus regius* or Hwass' *dominicanus.* Recent research at Harvard and the Smithsonian tends to support this view. What's your opinion?"

Thoroughly discredited in the eyes of his fellows who are now laughing at *him,* he turns as pink as the throat of a Queen Conch (or *Strombus gigas* as we pedants say). "Give her your opinion, Joe," his friends urge, making haste to buy a Tiger Cowry (35¢) or a paperback book ($1.) to show that they, at least, are on the side of the angels. Some of my most joyous moments are spent demolishing Joes.

However, anyone who shows proper respect and receptivity is treated gently; even people who argue with me, insisting that the shape of a shell is determined by the motion of the ocean. After all, how do I know to what degree they may be right? I know only that many forces besides the pull of tides have built these marvels.

There is the pull of heredity, as strong as or stronger than that of environmental surroundings. In obedience to his genes each mollusk constructs his shell to specifications, as accurately as though he were following a set of blueprints.

It comes as a shock to many people that an animal is involved at all; their surprise always comes as a shock to me. These are the molded-by-waves theorists, who believe that shells are actually mineral deposits or the calcified remains of vegetation. They repeat "animal" numbly after me, obviously visualizing something with four legs and a tail, totally lost. It is hard for some people to think of an oyster or a snail as an "animal," but then it is hard for some people to classify themselves in that category.

Some people will go along with "animal," yet persist in thinking that the shell was its "house," a place of habitation it found fully developed, with plumbing installed and bearing a vacancy sign. I suppose we can thank our friend the hermit crab, that busy little subleaser of abandoned shells, for this popular misconception; but the poets must share part of the blame. Calling a mollusk's shell his house is more poetry than truth. It was no more his house than your skeleton is your house. You built the skeleton to your specifications; it grew as you grew and made room for you. He used a different set of blueprints, and you needn't sulk because he ended up with something prettier.

Look at a shell, or a picture of a shell: not all of it, just at the tiniest, topmost portion from which the rings start to widen. That was the beginning. That was, and is, it as a baby. Once the animal was small enough to fit in there; eventually, it needed more space. The soft parts—the mantle—secreted a limy substance and began building, with an eye not only to the present but to the future.

A shell is no ramshackle, jerrybuilt construction of packing crates and bailing wire. It is easy to see how the concept of "houses" got started, because shells are architectural wonders. Take the pink Queen Conch, which almost everyone has seen. When it is a baby, a child, and a teen-ager it is called a "roller" because the shell will roll if placed on its side since it has grown only around and around in descending spirals from the spire. Then, when the time is ripe, it spreads its wing, building a flaring lip, anchoring it to the already existing framework.

SHE SELLS SEASHELLS

While this is apparent in the Queen Conch, or *Strombus gigas,* it is even more startling in another member of that family, *Strombus latissimus,* in which the lip goes all the way up and over the top, solidly framing the snail's youthful efforts, like a treasured picture of the creature when young.

Did I hear someone say "snail?" Didn't I tell you? All the gastropods, or univalves, are snails. The bivalves are clams, oysters, scallops, or mussels, to leave it in the simplest terms. And then there are the Cephalopods, the Tusk Shells, the Chitons, the Monoplacophora, but we don't want to go over our heads in this first lesson, do we?

I just want to touch on the matter of age, since people are always asking me "How old is this shell?" This question is difficult to answer since so few species have been kept under observation for long periods of time in captivity. Observing them by periodic visits to their habitats proves little, since it is difficult to recognize "John" or "Alice" with any reasonable certainty that it is the same John or Alice seen last time. The relative sizes of shells within a species may tell us which is older and which is younger, but comparisons between shells of different species tell us nothing. They grow at different rates of speed, like dogs. A Chihuahua and a Great Dane may celebrate their birthdays together, but the little fellow will never be eye-to-eye with the big fellow as long as he lives. This is as true with a genus or super-family, as it is of shells in general. To pursue the analogy with dogs, one cannot rest secure in the belief that all terriers are small and all setters are large. It would be nice if one could say that all little shells are cowries and all big ones are cones, but that's not the way things are. Each genus that is composed of a fair number of species comes in a variety of sizes. Let's stay with *Strombidae*

—pardon my Latin, but as the plural it does sound better than Strombuses, doesn't it? Among the more than eighty members of this family we have a range from a runt like *minimus* to a giant like *goliath*. And believe me, if all names were as self-explanatory as those I would have a lot less trouble writing this book.

Let's get one thing settled. *I* know that *minimus* isn't the smallest *Strombus* extant, even though Linné thought it was when he named it back in 1771. I know that the lightweight title among *Strombidae* is currently held by *Strombus helli,* which was found in 1844 and is commonly called Hell's Conch, but who the heck cares? Every statement one can make about shells is so hemmed in by qualifying "ifs," "ands," and "buts" that if one were to observe all contra-contradictions, one could never finish a simple declarative sentence, much less a book. A certain amount of latitude is essential. The conspiracy against seashells has grown fat on just such confusion.

So I would be grateful if the smart alecks in the corridor would hold their tongues. Even experts make mistakes. I've heard them. Furthermore—oh rapture!—I've heard them admit it.

The truth of the matter is that so few of the answers are known that anybody's lucky guess might mean a breakthrough. A couple of friends of mine, George and Dorothy Raeihle (he's a past president of the New York Shell Club; she is the editor of our "Club Notes") discovered that *Strombus pugilis,* the Fighting Conch, had been much maligned by the famous authority Linné, who christened it in 1758. The Raeihles collect not only shells but the living animals as well, and have kept several alive for long periods in small aquaria in their home. Lately they acquired a *S. pugilis* who surprised

ly in error, and missed an opportunity to b
travel. Asiatic oysters look nothing like the las
n the half-shell.

fference! One of the most exciting things about
r geographical distribution. A certain species may
n Heron Island in the Great Barrier Reef off
ut nowhere else. You need not expect it to wash up
sland after a storm, no matter how severe.

ural habitat is a basic fact about shells that prac-
ody knows, thanks to the conspiracy. Many a collec-
s day at the New York World's Fair ruined by the
e of the wrong shells in the right pavilions. To a
gist the sight of a Hawaiian warrior blowing on
Indian conch or a Javanese appropriating as his
Mississippi River Shell is anathema. Only the Filipinos
along specimens from their home grounds; but these
pt under the counter (the proper place for things in
no one is interested). Several smart collectors made
ood buys at the Philippine Pavilion.

intain a running battle with photographers who want,
e it's pretty, to rent an unsuitable shell from me. When
o-Pacific Triton's Trumpet appears in a photograph of
yland beach, it is not because I did not try to prevent it.
ly last week I lost a sale because I would not assure the
cer of a film that there were shells common to both
s of this country. He was making an industrial docu-
tary that was to include a beach scene. So that no one
t feel offended, this was to be Everyman's beach, with
ing in the fauna to single out Maine or Florida, New-
t, Rhode Island, or Newport Beach, California. I had to tell
n there was no such shell, except possibly that of a scallop,

them by being not a pugilist but a pacifist. He wasn't even carnivorous, timidly emerging to eat his algae after his smaller associates had picked all the meat off it.

Even then, if a tiny *Neritina* looked at him crosseyed, he would retreat into his shell until everyone else was gorged and asleep. *Strombus pugilis,* indeed! *Strombus ferdinandus* would be more suitable.

Incidentally, *Strombus* and its close cousin, *Lambis,* or Spiders, are the only ones who can properly be called conchs; although *Pleuroploca gigantea,* the Florida Horse Conch, has been called one for so long that it is too late to stop. I find that people who have just inched past the point of calling every shell a shell tend to call them all conchs.

"Do you carry conchs?" they ask on the telephone. "Yes," I used to say confidently. They would grab a cab and rush over, and then be furious at me because I did not have what they wanted. Now I ask them to be more explicit, explaining that "conch" basically means "shell"—hence "conchology," the study of shells—and inquire just what they have in mind. Is it pink? Is it brown? Or, perhaps, white?

Often it's the white Giant Clam shell, which was the architectural inspiraton for a much photographed hotel in Puerto Rico called "La Concha" (which, in Spanish, simply means "the shell"). Using "conch" that way is an understandable mistake, but there has of late been an amazing new trend. Three apparently unassociated people have harassed me lately by asking for abalones when they wanted Giant Clams. Those two species could not have less in common in color and shape.

How this particular confusion began I shall never know. I do, however, find it encouraging because it means that somewhere someone dropped a name, and others were sufficiently impressed to emulate him. So, all right, it was the wrong name. But at least it was a beginning, an awareness that shells do have names of their own. It's the first rung of the ladder.

To recapitulate: you and I may have a little trouble telling a *Tridacna* (clam) from a *Haliotis* (abalone), but Brother Mollusk knows from the very start who he is and makes his plans accordingly.

Class dismissed.

Back in my traveling days, could no longer run and pla taken better advantage of tho visits in foreign lands. In Jap India, instead of drooling over t should have asked the way to the would have seen *Strombus* and nating mollusks being sold as fo Malone used to advertise her ware thought that cockles and mussels, were the only mollusks fit for huma monotonously alike in appearance a

which has a way of superficially resembling its brethren everywhere. I showed him two or three, only to be told that was the one shell that could not be used. He and his confreres had ruled it out in advance on the ground that a scallop shell was the trademark of a certain industrial giant and the specific industrial giant who was paying for this film might resent the intrusion of a plug for a competitor. So much for *Pectinidae,* a world-wide group of several hundred species that were all typecast, and linked forever in the public mind with you-know-what.

The producer decided he would be safer with something ubiquitous like sand and driftwood, rather than running the risk of some know-it-all in the audience recognizing a New England Neptune and bragging about it. He bought nothing, but I didn't mind too much because he, for one, believed me. Most persons in his position think I am merely being stuffy if I try to steer them right, to keep them from making fools of themselves in the eyes of that one in ten who knows.

I behave this way only when I am told that the picture must be ambiguously general or authentically specific. If it's to be a fanciful shot, as most of them are, then the sky's the limit. Shells can be mixed in those gorgeous bouquets to which they so aptly lend themselves, as I display them in the shop, or as I arrange them in my home, without discrimination as to point of origin or ancestry.

It is simply that I do not want to be party to the perpetuation of the myth that shells are the same the world over. One of the best articles on the subject ever written, itself a collector's item, appeared in the *National Geographic* magazine of July, 1949. Its author, Rutherford B. Platt, aptly titled it "Shells Take You Over World's Horizons."

SHE SELLS SEASHELLS

I made a vicarious journey via seashells one night in January of 1965, rummaging through someone else's steamer trunk, in the midst of New York's transit strike when nobody could go anywhere. Many people found the shop during that strike because they passed it on foot instead of being underground in a subway or oblivious on a bus. It was touching to see their tired faces light up as they stopped to look in the window. People smiled at that window, as they do at those of pet shops, recognizing something natural and lovable that belongs to us all. Many interrupted their forced marches to wander in, to stare, smile, and react with excitement to what they saw. One such person was Barbara Reynolds.

Her opening remark, "Do you buy shells?", was one of which I have grown very tired. In the first place, the remark is so incredibly stupid. Do people think I acquired the inventory of my shop for free by snorkling, scuba diving, or dredging all over the world in the proper season for each particular shell; which, with the subsequent time necessary for cleaning, packing, and shipping home, would make me, roughly, about 210 years old? Or are they so unknowing as to think that I replenish my stock weekends from the sands of Fire Island, painting them in the evenings to produce an exotic and wholly fraudulent effect? Nobody asks the proprietress of a stocking store if she personally knitted every pair, but many people ask me if I "picked up" all these shells. (Some come from two hundred and seventy-five fathoms down!) Many are sure I paint them, and one benighted soul even asked me if I had *made* all of them myself! This is one hazard of being in a business that hardly anyone understands. But do I buy shells? Do I buy SHELLS? Just ask my accountant.

For most people who ask the question it is a spur-of-the-moment thing. They have come upon the shop and suddenly dreamed great dreams of making money in their spare time. They will find shells just like those in my windows on Connecticut beaches and sell them to me for whatever they demand; or they have this little box of stuff that Grandpa brought back after World War I. Can't they see the difference? Don't they know that I cannot rely on the random passers-by, but must have regular suppliers of fresh material if I am running anything except a blind for a bookie joint? Most of my bad tempers are triggered by that question, "Do you buy shells?"

There's another type, the most maddening of all, who asks this question. That is the wise guy who is going to Jamaica for a vacation and wants a ten-minute cram course in conchology so he will know which shells to bother to look for and which are piker stuff to leave alone. He doesn't know that there are experienced shellers who have gone to Jamaica ten years in a row in pursuit of that elusive specimen. He doesn't know that "rare" means "hard to find," and that there are no price tags under the sea to guide him in his selection.

When I first became the owner of the shop I felt sorry for these poor misguided souls. Then their motivating force became apparent. It was greed, the desire to get something for what they consider nothing—the hitherto scuffed-away object on the beach, the contents of Grandpa's cigar box stored in the back of the closet, the idle hours spent scuba diving which might be converted to monetary gain. Most disturbing of all, their attitude implies contempt of shells, and to me "them's fighting words."

But to return to Mrs. Reynolds: she was different, although

I did not perceive that at once. I countered her gambit with my usual surly counter-question, "What kind of shells?"

"All kinds," she said. They all say that, even if they think that, at the most, "all kinds" mean three. But she went on to explain that her collection was the fruit of a five-year trip on a sailing yacht with her husband, an anthropologist, shells that they had either gathered themselves or had been given as honored guests of the islanders. I was interested.

Five years before the mast were etched on her lovely face; wisdom and understanding were in the sea-blue eyes. She had hoped, she said, to spend her declining years (still a while in the offing) cataloguing and studying her shells, although she knew, given her nature, that she would never have leisure in which to do so. She felt that Fate had timed her brief sojourn in New York to coincide with the transit strike so that she might walk past my shop and discover an unexpected source of funds.

Mrs. Reynolds was now living in Hiroshima, and working with the World Friendship Center for the rehabilitation of atomic-bomb victims. She was in this country to give a series of fund-raising lectures. The victims did not need money as charity but as working capital with which to buy materials to make into salable objects. This was Friday. She must leave the city on Monday morning. Would I buy her shells?

How could I resist? I tried to be the levelheaded merchant instead of giving way to sentiment.

"I suppose you have complete data," I said.

"Data?" she echoed, frowning. It was obvious she did not know what the word means to shell people.

To some collectors data is all. They want to know whether the shell was dredged, trawled, or taken by a diver, at what depth, near what landmark, on what date. If you can also furnish the diver's or fisherman's first name, so much the better. A museum will not accept a legacy of shells without data, and I have seen devout collectors resist specimens they are simply dying to have because I could give for points of origin only the general locality such as "Philippines" or "West Indies." The ones I wanted to buy from Mrs. Reynolds would have to be handsome enough to make it on their own with customers who are aesthetically motivated, unless she could supply enough history to satisfy the scientists.

I translated "data" for her, and to my relief she said, "You mean where they came from? Oh, yes, I have all that."

It was agreed that she would arrange to have the shells delivered to my apartment, next door to the shop, the following morning. I would look them over, decide if I wanted to buy them, and make an offer if I felt so inclined. We shook hands on the bargain, and she resumed her hike to Seventeenth Street.

On Saturday morning a nice Quaker gentleman appeared with an aluminum steamer trunk. I had time to unwrap only one or two shells before having to leave to open the shop; but at the end of the workday I got to play with the rest of them until nearly two o'clock Sunday morning. Very few were labeled. Mrs. Reynold's "data" was a list of the ports-of-call of her meandering odyssey. At first I felt completely disheartened, certain I would never be able to sort out and identify this welter of material in time to make her an intelligent offer only thirty-six hours later. Then, all at once, the shells were speaking to me. I had developed a skill that I did not even know I had. Like someone able to "hear" the Bach B Minor Mass by perusing the score, I was able to see the points of origin of these specimens. Island-hopping back and forth across the world I went to: Galápagos, Guadeloupe, New Guinea, Samoa, Sanibel, Yap, and Zanzibar, lovely Zanzibar. I saw palm trees and orchids and turquoise lagoons, as though I were there.

There were no rare shells in the lot but there were enough uncommon ones for me to make her a respectable offer. I'm sure it was more than she expected, for she seemed terribly happy about it when she came to pick up the trunk. Then back she went to her work in Hiroshima—one place in this wide world I would not like to see, even if only in my mind's eye.

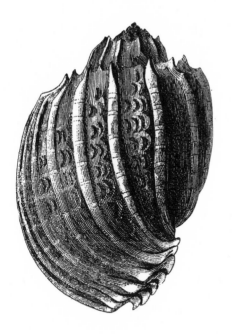

Five

Scared though I was on my first day as an employee, I was clam-cool compared to myself on June 24, 1964, when I had worked my way to the top. Now president of the company, I had achieved this eminence not by ordinary dint of diligence; nor had I married into the boss's family since, as you may remember, I was already a part of it. I owned my success simply to the fact that I could not say no.

Ten years had passed. During the first six of them, every Saturday was devoted to the McArthur Shop. Not for me the joys of a weekend in the country. Moreover, since the full-time shop assistant was a devout Orthodox Jew who observed even the most obscure religious holidays, many of my week-middles were preempted. I loved every minute of it. It fed my ego to know that I could sell more on a Saturday than the boss plus his assistant did the other five days of the week—I, who loathe selling and being sold to, or at.

My only previous sales experience had been at Macy's department store where, like many another female resident of New York City, I did a tour of duty. One of my friends describes Macy's as a foreign legion for women in which they serve as volunteers "to forget or be forgotten." This leaves out those dedicated souls who want to get somewhere in merchandising, and I seriously considered myself one of these until I flunked the secret-agent shopper's test in Suggestive Selling.

Suggestive Selling (which sounds dirty enough to get one in trouble with the authorities) means not merely being delighted that the customer has bought something, but making an effort to sell him or her something additional. When anyone tries it with me I coil back into my shell and slam my operculum. (An operculum is a trap door, sometimes called a "lid" or "foot," which, along with many other uses, mollusks have to insure privacy when they desire it. In some species it is vestigial and hides no more than would a band-aid on the Venus de Milo; in others it is attractive in itself. The green, brown, and white cat's-eye used in jewelry is the operculum of *Turbo petholatus,* the Tapestry Turban.

Handsome or scablike, an *operculum* is a must for the serious scientific collector, constituting with the shell the "hard parts" of the animal, the late lamented being called the "soft parts." Theoretically it is supposed to prove, if proof be needed, that the critter was live-taken, but in practice I don't see that it works out that way. From some suppliers I get shells with their presumed "percs" packed separately in a little box. Who am I to say which belongs to whom, or whether some of them are left over from last season's catch? I am supposed to select the proper perc, glue it on cotton, and then plug it in so the scientific collector will feel confident he is getting his money's worth; that he is buying a specimen "with operculum," or "w/O," as those in the know short-hand it. In practice I leave the percs right in the box unless it seems otherwise advisable, for it is my heretical belief that a shell looks prettier without one, especially if a highly-colored throat is one of its glories.

Besides, I weary of the comments. "Why'd you stick the cotton in that one?" "Ugh! That one's still got something in it. Can you take it out? I don't want to touch it." And most of my customers not only look at shells but audition them, testing the volume of the fabled ocean's roar. You can't hear a murmur in a shell that's swaddled in cotton. My shop might well be called "The Port of Lost Operculums.")

To resume, I found that suggestively selling shells was doing what comes naturally. I loved the darn things so much that I wanted to be sure that if someone saw one he liked, he would immediately be exposed to another. I always made certain, however, to leave him carfare.

The lack of sales resistance I encountered, coupled with the low rent of the shop on Sixty-first Street, made me feel that the shell business would be a veritable gold mine if every day were like my Saturdays. T'aint so, of course. Now each week is like a Saturday split six ways because, thanks to the dratted conspiracy, there are just so many people you can catch in a people-trap, despite the fact that there are hordes of unsuspecting people out there who would adore to join the fun if they could only be reached.

But I did not suspect this ten years ago when I told McArthur to think of me if he ever wanted to sell out or take on a partner. I wanted to get my hands on that shop, to run it as I knew it should be run. It was the woeful gulf between the potential goal and actuality that made me quit in despair after six years. Don't get me wrong. There was nothing *wrong* with the shop. It just lacked *umphhh*. It was a trap with no bait in it. Now I buy more "cheese" than I can afford, than I have room for, to keep it looking alive and limitless and always with a fresh surprise or two. This cuts deeply into the profits, but I believe it is the only way to run a shell store in New York City, where there are so many other things to engage people's interest.

Four years passed, during the first of which I was like a shellfish out of water. I missed the shop desperately but there was no turning back. I had truly slammed the door behind me when leaving. Short tempers, like reticence, run in the family. McArthur and I had simultaneously blown our stacks and uttered words that would be impossible to eat.

Time heals all, though, and necessity may be the mother of reconciliation, Suddenly, or so it seemed to me (although he might have been brooding on it for a long time), McArthur wanted to get out of the shell business. He remembered that I once had said I would like to get into it. He called me. To be precise, he had his assistant, Mr. Braun, call me. Fred Braun and I had remained friends; we had continued to exchange holiday greetings, and frequently bumped into each other and enjoyed long pleasant chats.

I never knew how old Braun was. People referred to him as

the "old man," to distinguish him from McArthur, who had to be in his late sixties as closely as I can figure it from family recollections. My cousin did appear to be the younger of the two, although Braun swore they were of the same age. True to his religion, Christian Science, McArthur would never reveal what that age was.

True to *his* religion, Orthodox Jewry, Braun always wore a hat in the shop. In winter it was a black homburg. His suit (suits?) was dark; the jacket cut a little longer than is customary. He always wore a vest, a white shirt, and a gray four-in-hand with a pearl stickpin. You could tell it was summer when he showed up in a Palm Beach suit and Panama hat with a black band. A good inch of thick wavy black hair showed beneath his hat brim.

He was sweet and friendly if he liked you. He had slaved for McArthur for twenty-five years, and the two of them bickered constantly. I'm told this grew even worse just before I went back into the shop, that they would not even interrupt their running argument to take care of a potential customer.

Braun had not only the appearance but the voice of an old-school Shakespearean actor. This voice issuing from my phone that day seemed but another segment in a dream, another echo from the past in the unreality through which I was passing. My mother had died the day before, after nearly two weeks in a coma.

Braun said that McArthur wanted to talk to me. I said I wasn't in very good shape to talk to anyone. I told him why. He expressed his sympathy and explained the situation to McArthur, who took the phone and expressed *his* sympathy. He said he wanted to discuss something with me, and I said I was not in a state of mind to discuss anything, that I would call him later in the week. He understood. He and his wife sent flowers.

There was so much to do, as there always is. I did it numbly, and the week inched by. McArthur called me before the end of it.

I was not yet able to think straight but he wanted me to make a quick decision about a matter that would alter my whole life. It had been a year for alterations, voluntary and involuntary. A major one had been the sale of a beloved white elephant, a two-hundred-year-old Connecticut farmhouse in which I could not afford to live and which I could barely support on the rental from tenants who were always finding new ways to spend my money. Having rid myself of that, did I now want to buy another elephant, perhaps even whiter?

My first response was a resounding no, followed by a tentative maybe, as the aptness of the timing struck me; at no other moment would I have been able to say yes if I so determined. Sale of the house had not only ended urgent demands upon my time and finances, but had provided the wherewithal to buy out McArthur. Furthermore, so rash an action would have caused my mother such distress that I doubt whether I would have even considered it during her lifetime.

Mother, poor darling, never had the slightest shred of confidence in herself nor any enterprise or person with whom she was remotely connected—like, for instance, a daughter. She always expected me to fall flat on my face, shunning school exercises if I had a line to recite, staying away from my piano teacher's musicales, and, much later, sitting with dripping hands beside her television set when a play based on a story I wrote was being shown for the third time, no doubt apprehensive that this time the reels would be reversed and the dialogue would come out backwards. I wasn't at all sure that I would be capable of running a store, but I knew that if I made a flop of it my mother would not be embarrassed.

McArthur said nothing about price, and I hadn't the vaguest notion as to what the figure would be. The only hint I could get was that he had asked another prospective buyer for $35,000, and been turned down. Braun, our go-between, told me that. He added that a relative could get it for a whole lot less.

I now know that $35,000 was exorbitant. No shell shop is worth half of that. On the other hand, a shell *collection* may be worth three times that much, or more. A Grade A collection is like a vintage wine cellar, containing items not available in the open market. Even though some of the wine may have lost its flavor, there will still be enough bottles of Napoleon brandy to justify the expense. Collections of that sort are bought by super-collectors who want to own them, to work over and catalogue them, to fit them in with what they already own. The only fate then ahead of a collection is ultimately to be sold to a super-super-collector or to be donated to a museum. No intelligent shopkeeper would buy a collection unless he planned to act only as a broker, selling it in its entirety to somebody else. Furthermore, that "somebody else," as well as two or three other highly likely prospects, had better be clearly in view before the purchase is made.

To put it another way, no small shell shop should carry an inventory worth in excess of $20,000 at any given moment if it wants to stay alive. It would be like stocking one's larder with only cream puffs, leaving no room for substantials like bread and milk. What would one eat for breakfast—toasted cream puffs?

Mind you, I'm talking only about inventory, not the intangible and unmeasurable value of a shop summed up in the term "good will." This involves past relationships with customers and suppliers, and one cannot arbitrarily put a price tag on these. I set these words down so that I will never have to eat those which preceded them. If I ever decide to sell the shop, I will be selling not only several thousand shells but my reputation and the blood and sweat that went into making it. I intend to charge dearly.

I didn't understand that then, I suppose because McArthur did not seem to have considered it either. Mr. X, to whom he had wanted to sell the shop, was a businessman who had not heretofore dabbled in offbeat enterprises, and he quite properly requested an inventory. My accountant keeps asking me for one, too, and I keep telling him that the only way I could take one would be if I did not do anything else, and under such circumstances how could I pay the rent? I might be able to complete one if I locked the door and cut off the phone for three months so that I would not be interrupted by customers —providing I did not go crazy within the first three weeks. Assuming I retained my sanity and completed the listing, the first busy Saturday after I reopened would blow the whole thing sky high.

For instance, take yesterday, when I was trying to satisfy three sets of customers simultaneously. The first was a science teacher and his two sons of about twelve and fourteen. Twelve needed examples of forty-three families of shells, most of which must be small enough to be glued in groups on cards, and all of which should not be costly. Fourteen was just after some eye-catching bargains for his cabinets. The second set consisted of a young collector (and I do mean young—seven years old that day, with birthday money burning a hole in his pocket); his baby brother, his mother, and a grandmother (upon whom an extra bite could always be put). The third set was a pair of newly-weds who had fallen in love with shells on their honeymoon in Nassau and wanted some for their table and oven as well as for their souls.

Juggling these three groups, which at times seemed to contain many more small boys than an actual inventory would show, I managed to round up and pack forty-three-plus shells for set number one, catered to little Mr. Gotrocks and his grandmother to the tune of $21, plus a buck for a bag of over a hundred shells for the tiny one to strew about, and satisfied the desire of the bride and groom to clutter up their new home. My stock of at least sixty species must have been diminished by one, but even in the cool calm of the Sunday after I was unable to say which.

Each shell had a Latin name, most of them unfamiliar to me, which ideally should have been on an alphabetical list somewhere about the place, but that would not have done any good since I could not recognize nor take the time to identify many of them, much less spell them well enough to find them on the list. The science teacher will spend many hours finding out what he bought; I will never know. The rich young collector had checked his acquisitions off his own list, and the couple was too much in love to care, so I did not write it all down explicitly in my salesbook because other customers who had gone for coffee until the crowd thinned out were coming back in. The record is lost beyond recall.

I suppose the trouble is that I have a literal mind with a yearning to be explicit. I am short on the ability to estimate roughly and would become a compulsive counter unless I curbed myself. Sure, I'd like to know how many *Olivella biplicata,* ½-inch, there are in a gallon, but I shall take care that I don't try to find out. Five-cent shells, by the very token of being five-cent shells, come in thousands. Maybe millions. Who knows? And who, besides my accountant and the Department of Internal Revenue, cares?

Let's face it: I care. It would give me great pleasure to know how much, to the penny, I make on a gallon of *O. biplicata,* but I'm too busy to indulge in such vagaries. I have another item, no bigger than a baby's little-piggy-nail, which I sell at 25¢ a scoopful. I know I paid too much for three pints of it, and I would like to know how much too much, but I might more successfully count the grains of sand on Sanibel Island.

Which suggests another method of taking inventory: categorizing by price rather than identification—for example, "5,000 50-cent shells, 300 $5 shells." The drawback to that method is that yesterday's five-dollar shell may be tomorrow's fifty-center or, more probably, vice versa. As the divers and fishermen become more sophisticated about seashells, they demand more for their catch. On the other hand, as diving and dredging equipment becomes more sophisticated, shells once considered rare may prove to be plentiful. Moreover, an inflationary spiral in a foreign country from which I buy can alter the picture.

McArthur had chosen to base Mr. X's requested inventory on the supposed retail value of each shell, which meant starting with the more expensive and obvious ones. In ten days, with three-quarters of the stuff still to be counted, he had reached the staggering sum of $18,000 so in his eyes Mr. X would be getting a bargain at $35,000. I may add that some of the costly but resistible items that heightened the total are still here, being resisted, while hundreds of new shells have come and gone.

Mr. X laughed, as well he might, when he heard the asking price. He must not even have thought it feasible as a starting point for bargaining since he made no counteroffer and left with a curt good-bye. That was when I came in.

I discussed the matter with only a few friends, being careful to select those who would not dismiss the whole thing as sheer folly. I did not wish to sow a crop of "I-told-you-so's" which I might bitterly have to harvest. I knew I was risking the chance of future "If-you-had-only-consulted-me's," but I stuck to the optimists among my coterie who would think it sounded like a lot of fun and importune me to do it.

Would the wet blanket of a pessimist have stopped me? I think it might have—cold. All the arguments a kill-joy might present I was already having with myself. I was over fifty. I had not had a job which entailed getting up every morning, getting dressed, and going to work since my twenties. To make the outlook worse, in the shop I would have to do it six days a week. Was I up to it physically, or had the self-indulgences of being a free-lance writer made me too soft, too indolent for such pursuits?

Not to mention my probable mental inadequacies. What made me think I knew enough about shells to drive shrewd bargains for their purchase throughout the world? Sure, I'd sold them, but buying was a mystery to me.

Leaving aside the peculiar demands of this tricky merchandise, did I think I had the business acumen necessary to run even a newstand? Would I buy high and sell low, and overload my inventory with clinkers? Would I remember to collect sales tax, record it, and keep enough money in the bank to pay it over to the proper authorities on the date it was due and not three days later?

Could I, who loathe wrapping packages and consider visits to the post office as nightmares, ever satisfy the demands of my far-flung clientele, a complication that does not plague the proprietor of a newsstand?

Many as were the known dangers, there were certainly unknown ones. The woods were full of them, and there was doubt that I could reach Granny's house without being eaten alive. So I clutched my little basket and whistled a happy tune to Helen, to Natalie, and others, knowing they would urge me to go ahead bravely.

Then I inadvertently told a certain Dorothy, who unnerved me by bringing up an argument I had not foreseen. How, she asked, could I be sure that the 1964 model of me would still enjoy the shop one day a week, much less six days? There had been a lot of water over the dam and under the bridge since I had last blithely waded in it. I had inevitably changed. The shell-buying public might also have changed. Quite possibly I would find the whole thing an unmitigated bore.

There was wisdom in this. I called McArthur not as a buyer or nonbuyer of his shop, but as a timid applicant for my old job as part-time assistant. For once in my life I was going to be sensible.

Six

It must have been three years since I had seen the shop; time had not dealt kindly with it. It seemed dingy and cluttered, a claustrophobe's nightmare; I suspected my doubting friend might be right, that I would find myself not liking it any more.

I had never liked this new location as much as the old and had tried to argue McArthur out of choosing it when he had to make way for the bulldozers on Sixty-first Street. For one thing, I thought it would be no time at all before he would have to move again, and moving the contents of a shell store is, believe me, no picnic.

Number 590 Third Avenue, in the middle of the block, was

perched on the edge of an excavation that extended to Thirty-eighth Street. (This excavation, by the way, was later to become the handsome apartment house in which I now reside.) Number 590 had been renovated, but its three neighbors to the north were, and still miraculously are, like a hag's remaining choppers, doomed to rapid extraction.

These were the early gold-rush days on Third Avenue. As soon as demolition of the "El" was completed in 1956, the boom was on. Speculators were buying, holding, and selling property, and the figures bandied around were astronomical. It is now my fervent hope that the owners of those three doomed teeth had held on a little too long and asked for too much, making their sale impossible; but when we moved in I expected our tenure to be merely a matter of months. Frankly, I hoped it would be no longer than that. Some of our old customers continued to find us, arriving with an air of triumph as though they had fought their way through fire and ice; but there were fewer surprises on Saturdays. The tempo had changed from upbeat to down.

I now love the location, and hope never to have to move, even though I could use twice as much space. I know that memory plays tricks, but mine is overdoing it because I can't remember the place, at the very beginning, looking as new and bright and alive as it now does each morning. I redecorated. I keep it clean and tidy and filled with beautiful things. However, I made so few physical changes there is only one possible explanation of why it is living now although it was "dead on arrival": the street where it lives has breathed life into it.

Once dreary old Third Avenue really swings. There are all of these big office buildings with thousands of potential shell lovers working in them. There's the Airlines Terminal, practically around the corner, through the portals of which pass other potential shell lovers from all points of the compass. Even motherly old Grand Central Station seems nearer because a living organism is ambulatory and thinks nothing of walking a couple of crosstown blocks. What used to be a dead end is now the crossroads of the world.

Pure luck. I don't think McArthur had a crystal ball that showed him how things would be in seven or eight years. I'm not even sure he would have enjoyed the forecast and risked its coming true, for it seems an odd coincidence that he wanted to pull out just as life began around him.

The shop as it was when I re-entered it in 1964, was an anachronism, a moribund musty-dusty museum piece. It looked dead, and the lively passers-by could only wonder why it did not volunteer for burial. It was a joke, something to snicker at. Now I have them laughing out of the other sides of their mouths for joy.

At the risk of sounding grand I must say that I believe the time was ripe for me to take over. The people, who now have the kind of shell shop they want, willed that I do so; if I had not existed they would have had to invent me.

As with all apparently mystical experiences, there is a practical, mundane explanation: to wit, McArthur felt the quickening of life around him and did not like it. He had a dwindling number of old customers; the few new ones adventurous enough to cross that depressing threshold wanted things to be different, for all the world as though the shop belonged to them instead of to him.

For one thing, they wanted the place to smell better. The first whiff of the air inside must have provoked many a quick, and permanent, exit. Because it did not offend him McArthur permitted an ancient and ailing cat to reside under the radiator beneath the shopwindow, and he saw no reason why her presence should offend anyone else.

He and Braun did their best, but the cat had unfortunately chosen the spot most difficult to clean. They kept putting fresh sand into cardboard boxes that had a tendency to disintegrate, dispersing the contents into unreachable corners. Now and again they would remove the soggy cardboard, placing it and whatever they could shovel off the tops of the dunes into a large trash container to await weekly collection. Then, more sand and another blotting-paper cardboard box.

There was another complication. Susie, the cat, would eat only raw pork liver, but, being senile, would not eat all of it when served, squirreling bits away in her lair where she forgot about them—though no one else could. Her oversight, taken advantage of by the first few invading cockroaches, caused their tribes to increase and flourish into the boldest bunch of bugs in New York City. Braun, unofficially in charge of the extermination of vermin, hated roaches so much that he wouldn't go near enough to step on one, nor would he use a spray or powder lest it harm Susie, whom he adored. Meeting no resistance, and not sensing that they were not welcome, the roaches colonized every corner of the shop, swarming inside the cabinets among the cowries and cones.

Let us take a hypothetical case: Mary Jones, who has somewhere got an inkling that seashells might be fun, enters the shop. She does not know the extenuating circumstances concerning Susie and assumes that some, perhaps not all, shells and marine specimens smell bad. Maybe, she thinks, it's because so many of them are housed here: a half dozen or so in her home would not do it any harm.

SHE SELLS SEASHELLS

Bravely, breathing as infrequently as possible, she advances. A drawer of a cabinet stands provocatively open. She enjoys what is in it, closes it, and opens the next one down. A thundering herd of roaches, disturbed in their slumber, stampedes in all directions. That settles it. She closes the drawer and that chapter of her life. Seashells are not fun. They smell bad and attract roaches. Who needs them?

Is it any wonder that the clientele did not increase in numbers?

The only customers were those so committed to shells that they were willing to endure anything to satisfy their craving. They convinced themselves that the shop was quaint and the two old codgers Dickensian, but even these diehards were soon demanding more of McArthur than he was willing to give. They wanted fresh delights, not the same old specimens week after week. The shop came to seem like a dull marriage.

What with old friends becoming disenchanted and potential new ones being repelled, things had reached a pretty impasse. The shop smelled of failure as well as of Susie, and I wasn't sure I would be able to tolerate either odor. And yet, I could not say no.

April 10, the day of my revisit, was an exciting one for me in another compartment of my life. A short story of mine, "The Gentleman Caller," was to be done that evening on television on *The Alfred Hitchcock Hour,* with Ruth McDevitt and Roddy MacDowell in leading roles. I had opening-night jitters, but this was the only day during the week that I could squeeze in a visit to the shell shop.

Our business discussion was vague and not to the point. McArthur would not say what he wanted for the kit and caboodle, except that it would be less than the $35,000 he had asked of the nonrelative. This left a lot of open water. I almost got the feeling that he would be willing to pay me to be rid of the place. He obviously wished I would stop shilly-shallying so that he could catch the next train home to Westchester with a signed statement in his pocket, springing him forever from durance vile. He winced when I told him I proposed to spend a couple of months not as a shilly-shallyer but as a researcher in depth. I would like to work in the shop for three full days each week, in order to ascertain whether I would be able to take double that amount of time.

"Talk it over with Braun," he said, slipping into his topcoat. "Fix up your schedules the way it suits both of you. It makes no difference to me." He put on his hat, saying if he did not leave this minute he would miss the 3:15.

Bankers' hours, I thought. After he had gone I learned from Braun that 3:15 P.M. was practically the middle of the night to McArthur. He had remained in Manhattan until this ungodly hour because of his appointment with me. He usually headed for home before noon, having attended to all the phases of his business that required his attention in the interval since his arrival at nine A.M., leaving Lieutenant Braun in full command of the operation—if there happened to be any. This put things in a different light. If I came muscling in, throwing my weight around and demanding three days of employment, I would be taking the bread, such as it was, out of Braun's mouth.

In the old days Braun had given the shop but two hours of his day, leaving the rest of it free to pursue his major interest—the buying and selling of paintings and other objects d'art. I had noted on entering that he had aged considerably, but so had everything else: the fixtures, the linoleum on the floor, even the shells. And, besides, he had always seemed old. Focusing my attention on him now, I could have wept. The hair curling beneath the black homburg was silver, the wrinkles deep, and the motions slow. He was clearly not up to trudging the streets in search of a random Rembrandt and, worse, had obviously given up hoping to find one. Before, I had believed his assertions that he was losing money every hour he worked for McArthur, perhaps missing bargains in the marts of art that would have made him a wealthy man. At some point, since I last checked in, he had abandoned pie in the sky for the safe harbor of the shell shop. Would he be able to manage without his wages, picayune though they were?

I could not come out and ask him an insulting question like that, but somewhere among my circumlocutions he must have heard a hint of it, for he was soon his jaunty former self, telling me he would welcome more freedom from the devotion and loyalty to McArthur that had kept him in bondage.

I compromised, saying I would take the afternoon trick twice a week, coming in at one o'clock. None of that nine-o'clock-in-the-morning nonsense for me. Who is in a mood to sell, or buy, seashells at nine o'clock in the morning? He could continue to come in and overlap with McArthur at his customary hour on those days, and have the field to himself on the three others. I would work all day on Saturdays, which once were my very own.

Another hitch developed. It seemed there was a third man involved in this enterprise (the income from which could barely feed a single bird), a man of mystery whom I shall call "John Doe." Doe lived in New England and was regularly employed throughout the week in some unknown capacity. Every Friday night he had to drive his boss to New York where he didn't have a thing in the world to do until boss-pick-up time on Sunday evening. Since he liked seashells, how better could he kill Saturday than by working in the shop? He had assumed permanent possession of the day.

Doe and Braun loomed as a pair of albatrosses if I bought the place, and Susie made three, not to mention the uncountable cockroaches. They had squatters' rights. The shop belonged to them, not, as I thought it should, to those impatient people outside who wanted it to be pretty and sweet-smelling. There was a struggle between the insiders and outsiders, a tug of war between death and life. I knew which side I wanted to win, yet I kidded myself that I could take up the challenge or leave it alone.

With Saturdays denied me I knew that two four-hour periods a week would in no way test my mettle for the long pull, especially if there were nothing to do but twiddle my thumbs. I'd been in there two and a half hours now, talking to McArthur and/or Braun, and not another living soul had ventured into this beyond.

I could have magnanimously offered to work for free on the days that Braun was there and getting paid, but I doubted that he would go for that, and I knew darn well that McArthur would not go for double salaries. Moreover, I knew even better that I would not at all like being in the shop with Braun. Dearly though I loved him, and still do although he would be the last to believe it, there is something so depressing about his ponderous mien that it makes looking at shells seem too close to "viewing the remains." If Braun was there, I knew I would be reduced to screaming madness in no time at all.

And, besides, it would not be a proper test. Finding out whether I still liked being in the shop meant finding out if I

[52]

liked being there alone, when I could be myself. Dearly though I loved him, etc., I could not be myself with Braun because he was so overpowering. He set the tone, and I would have to dance to his tune. With him I would feel self-conscious being myself.

More then that. I am aware of my limitations of character, and I knew if he were there I would cheat, letting him wrap the more exasperating packages, ducking the boring customers who are right up his alley, and grabbing the interesting ones as my own. That halfway experiment would not prove a thing.

So it was decided that I would work, totally alone, three afternoons a week, starting Monday.

If you think New York City air is atrocious, you should have sniffed it that Friday in April after three hours in the old McArthur Shop. Pure ambrosia!

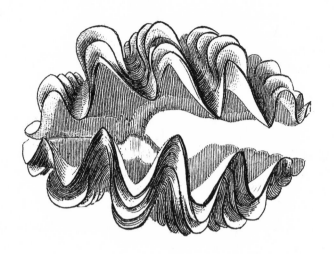

Seven

During the first three lonely afternoons I tried to brush up on seashells and was appalled to discover how much I had to learn, to relearn, and, as I was later to discover, in some cases unlearn. As I have said, much of the stock that remained was dregs, rejects dating back a quarter of a century. The names on their yellowing labels were not necessarily the ones they answered to now, and some had not been right in the first place.

I know of no really satisfactory way to label shells in a shop. McArthur's method was to type over and over and over again, making four carbon copies at a time, some such finger twister as *Nomaeopelta mesoleuca,* Menke, 1851, Guaymas, Sonora, Mexico, 25¢. Try that on your hunt-and-peck system, or even if you are a Katherine Gibbs graduate, try to do it impeccably twenty-five times. This shell is a one-inch green-blue limpet. Limpets are the ones called Chinese Hats, and all of these were overtrimmed with printed matter. A box full of them looked like a rat's nest.

The only dependable way to keep shell and label together is to bind them with some bulldog adhesive such as porcelain cement (as McArthur did) and let the buyer worry about prying them apart when he gets them home. If he telephones for advice as to how to get rid of the shred of paper and the gob of cement, recommend nail-polish remover and hang up quickly.

Such a method would not do for me. There is a mutual attraction between me and adhesives that makes it impossible for me even to put a stamp on a letter without getting sticky. I never will understand how those ladies with a passion for gluing shells on things manage. I would have to spend most of my time washing up.

So what else could one do? What would I do if I bought the place, having listened so sympathetically for years to people's gripes about removing McArthur's labels. I promised myself that I would not let them grumble so about me.

Neither Scotch tape nor those miraculous little stickers, like beauty spots, which are guaranteed to adhere to anything, work on shells that do not have a suitable surface, and so few of them do. Loose labels in an envelope, kept in the same compartment as the shells they identify, are not the answer since they have a tendency to go compartment hopping with the aid of some eager looker and wind up in the wrong pew.

With bivalves you can put a folded label inside like a fortune in a cookie. The trouble with bivalves, however, is that they are truly "bi-" by the time they reach a shell shop. What keeps them together in life is a muscle or a ligament, living matter that dries and deteriorates after the animal is removed. This comes as a great surprise to people who expect them to open and close like pillboxes.

The hinges of bivalves are wondrous things and should not be overlooked. Some of them are ball-and-socket arrangements which must have inspired the earliest engineers. Some are exactly like zippers, with precise interlocking teeth.

Which reminds me. I have a customer who is a dentist. For three months he bought not for himself but for a friend who was a "shell nut." He came in every week, made his selections, but remained immune to infection with the fever himself. Then, one day, I sold him a *Glycymeris gigantea*. This is a chubby brown-and-white clam from West Mexico, which is lovely either buffed to a porcelain-like lustre or left rough *au naturel*. If the valves become separated, infinite patience is required to get them back together again since the teeth and the spaces between them dovetail with their counterparts like pieces of a jigsaw puzzle.

Doctor Smith returned the next morning, obviously upset. He told me that something terrible had happened. Thinking he had dropped the shell and broken it, I hastened to reassure him, explaining that I had recently received a shipment and had plenty of others on hand. That was good, he said, because otherwise he would have had to make another selection for his friend. Now that *Glycymeris* and he had found each other, no third party would be permitted to come between them. Her perfect occlusion had won his professional heart and worn down his resistance. Having embraced her, he yielded to suppressed desires to possess shells himself instead of giving them to another; he went on a full-blown spree, buying three cowries, a cone, and a murex. The shell bug, so long held at bay, had bitten deeply, again with perfect occlusion, which I hadn't thought bugs had.

If only someone with the doctor's enthusiasm had come in during those first three sessions or those in the two weeks that followed! The gloom got me down. I crept home to lonely evenings, avoiding friends who would be sure to sense the change in me and tell me to stop whatever it was I was doing. The only thing that kept me going was the shells and a fanatic conviction that there was need for a shop selling them in New York City. It wasn't easy to keep the faith, observing how blithely the City ignored the shop that had been in existence for many years.

It had been started by the late Christine McArthur, Mc-Arthur's first wife. They had lived in Florida during the boom in the mid-1920s. Following in his mother's footsteps, Mc-Arthur was in real estate—but who was not in Florida real estate, to some degree, in those bonanza days? It was said that every bootblack in Manhattan owned a bit of *terra* there that was *firma* when the tide was out. Acreage was bought over the breakfast table and sold for a tidy profit before lunch. Many people made killlings. Crosbie McArthur did not.

I shall always regret not having known Christine. Everyone who did adored her. They remember her exquisite taste and the knack she had for making others, previously blind to it, see the beauty in seashells.

She had discovered them while everyone else was engaged in the frenzy of buying and selling land. I see her as a little detached from it all, strolling the beaches, finding these solacing things, at first thinking of them only as materials with

[57]

which to make pretty place cards and jewelry, then becoming more deeply involved, wondering about them, and reading whatever was available to answer some of her questions.

Actually, I think I did see her once. A long while ago, she had a booth at the annual Flower Show in New York's old Grand Central Palace, up on the third or fourth floor where all the garden gadgets and maple sugar patties were sold. I am always tired when I reach that section, even in the new Coliseum, but I vaguely recall a table spread with necklaces and earrings fashioned of seashells. It may be imagination in retrospect, but I think I noticed a sign proclaiming these to be the work of Mrs. Crosbie D. McArthur, and thought, "Isn't that the name of that cousin of mine I met when I was six years old in Cleveland?" But I did not speak to the small gentle woman of the possible relationship. I did not care for shell jewelry. I was a sophisticated youngster in that era of F. Scott Fitzgerald, and it took a diamond as big as the Ritz to engage my interest.

The more fool I, muffing an opportunity to shake her hand. I remain forever in her debt for my shop, and I might at least have said hello.

Other visitors to the show were not so blasé. I have since learned that Christine did a land-office business and took enough orders back to Florida with her to keep her gluing for months. This warm and lucrative welcome given her by the big town influenced the McArthur's decision after the land boom had undeniably become a bust. The young couple cut their ties with the sunny South and moved to New York.

Armed with an impressive list of local clients and her own sweetly stubborn determination, Christine was able to talk Brentano's Book Store into letting her have a corner in which

SHE SELLS SEASHELLS

to sell—of all things—seashells and things made of seashells. McArthur opened an antique shop in a darling little enclave of shops which used to grace Third Avenue somewhere in the forties and was later displaced by a parking lot.

I'm sorry I cannot be more accurate about dates. The habit of record-keeping was introduced into my bloodstream by my British grandfather who was related to McArthur only by marriage, and I cannot be held responsible for anything that happened before I got in on the act. I do know that Christine sold shells in Flushing, New York, during the second summer of the 1939–1940 World's Fair. I went out there every week and thought I knew every inch of the fair grounds. I never once passed her booth. Some time, between then and 1954, she died.

I think it was chiefly as a tribute, a memorial, to her that McArthur sold his antiques and took over her shell shop. He claimed it was easier to dispose of antiques, but perhaps there was more to that than meets the eye. Christine loved shells. She wanted to make them available to other people who would love them too. From all I have heard of her she would have wanted her shop to endure, like a shell, after she had vacated it.

I would be the last to deny that her sweetly stubborn wraith was still active in 1964, making new arrangements because her widower no longer wanted to mind the store. Perhaps I never had the slightest chance of not taking up the burden. Can you think of a better explanation?

After three miserable weeks during which I ferreted out all the facts a potential seller keeps from a potential buyer, I sold a bloc of A.T.&T. stock and bought the place. Though it no longer bears her name, Christine's shell still endures.

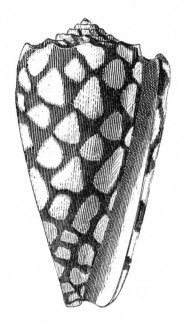

Eight

Although few people were buying shells, interest in them was not exactly dormant. Some person, or persons unknown, was or were stealing them on a regular basis. A certain amount of pilferage might be expected. Some children, and even a few grownups, can't get over the idea that a shell is something you find, something you pick up, and that anyone who prefers to sell it to you because she found it and picked it up first is simply interfering with God's Law. The hanky-panky that had been going on in McArthur's shop, however, was the work not of amateurs but of highly skilled pros, who soiled their hands with only the most valuable shells, such as a Golden Cowry and a *Voluta bednalli*.

SHE SELLS SEASHELLS

The Golden Cowry Caper was a beaut, involving the tactic of the switcharoo. Neither Braun nor McArthur knew for how many weeks a modest Tiger Cowry (35¢) had masqueraded in the rare shell case as a *Cypraea aurantium* ($200 and up), so cleverly was it disguised by several coats of orange lacquer. Some innocent-seeming customer must have memorized the features and color of the real McCoy, fashioned a duplicate, and returned to the shop to make the substitution.

Famous last words: this could never happen to me. I really don't believe it could—not with a Golden Cowry, but so far I have had only one in the shop since I've owned it, and vigilance was my watchword every minute of the three weeks it was there.

By no means the most expensive of the genus, I would nominate the Golden Cowry as the one most likely to be stolen. *Cypraea guttata,* the Rare Spotted Cowry, which every owner of a Tiger Cowry is certain he has whenever its name and price appears in print, has fetched as much as $4,000. Comparable sums have been paid for *C. leucodon* and *C. broderipi.*

Worth several hundreds of dollars is *Cypraea fultoni,* which is found only in the stomach of a bottom-feeding fish called a Mussel Cracker. Thousands of feet down in the waters off South Africa, this predator hunts for his favorite snack. The odds against getting a *C. fultoni* at all are stupendous, since every fisherman in the area must be sought out and taught to investigate the innards of any Mussel Cracker he finds in his net or dredge. The odds against getting one in prime condition are practically insurmountable. The fish's digestive juices attack the shell immediately upon ingestion, and unless he's caught very soon nothing will remain but a scarred fragment.

I have heard of a boy in Capetown whose desire to own a *C.*

fultoni became an obsession. He decided that waiting around for other fishermen to catch Mussel Crackers was too passive an approach, and that he would prefer to make personal contact at the very far end of a fishing rod. He devoted hours to planning his campaign, determining what sort of line would be strong enough to withstand the enormous pressure to which it would be subjected, what kind of weight would plummet the hook to its destination. The question of bait was an easy one to answer. Crackers fancied cowries, so the novelty of one from shallower waters would surely attract them. Then there was the question, which the boy worked out mathematically, as to the rate at which his line should be reeled in once he felt a tug on it. It must be done very slowly, with frequent pauses to allow the fish to adjust to changes in pressure. If done too fast, the fish might explode, and the cowry be lost forever.

I am happy to say that after a couple of years of persistent patience the boy finally got his *C. fultoni.* I don't know whether or not I'm happy to add that he eventually sold it, having risen to the bait of an offer so tempting that he was unable to resist it. I have not been told the sum, only that it was enough to enable him to finish college, where his principal subject was marine biology. I suppose the dream is the important thing, and seeing one's efforts capped with success. After all, he did it once, and lightning might, for once, strike again. I hope so.

Other species are also found only inside fishes; they are described as being *ex-pisces*. Some of them seem hardly worth the bother. They are an acquired taste, like olives, which is a ridiculous metaphor to use in this context since a taste for olive *shells* does not need to be acquired but is inevitable once the subject has been exposed to them. Olives, like cowries, have instantaneous appeal for anyone who likes bright, shiny surfaces that are smooth to the touch. They shine because the animals who built them burnished them constantly, wrapping themselves around the outside of their shells, spreading layers of enamel, like coats of nail polish, buffing until they gleamed. Some people do not approve of this, finding the result gaudy if not downright vulgar.

These people are in a minority, but they bother me. Usually they begin by berating me for taking a nice dingy shell like those they find on beaches and polishing it to a fare-thee-well. Some say they don't like them because they don't look real. I cannot fathom the workings of those minds at all.

Not real? What could be more real than a cowry or olive obeying its instincts and doing what comes naturally? And what could be more exciting in this age of fakery than something that doesn't *look* real, yet *is* instead of the usual vice versa? I get so darned mad every time some dame flutters her false eyelashes and denigrates cowries and olives because she is unable to believe in them.

Some people, like the magazine editor I once heard say that "a story was believable but it wasn't credible," will accept the fact that the shell was mollusk-, not man-made, only after I have backed up my opening remarks by showing them pictures in reputable scientific publications. Many excuse their disbelief by saying that the shell looks just like porcelain, which cues me in to one of my favorite anecdotes.

It seems that Marco Polo was an instant cowry lover who brought a few home in his pocket as souvenirs of his first expedition to China. He also brought back the first crockery from that country to have been seen in Italy. Italians went wild over the shells. To one whimsical viewer they resembled sleek, chubby baby pigs; he nicknamed them *porcelanas,* their word for little porkers. When interest shifted to the more practical things Marco had brought, such as dishes, people were amazed to discover that these were just as shiny as the shells and so different from commonplace pottery that they deserved to be called something else.

What else? Almost every day someone remarks upon the resemblance of cowries to porcelain. Way back then, someone phrased it the other way round.

The Italians still call *Cypraea* "porcelanas," and the French say "porcelaines." How did we get stuck with an ugly, unevocative word like "cowries"? To make it worse, someone who was unaware of the trickiness of English spelling wrote the singular as "cowrie," which is like calling one of a group of ladies a "ladie." Only one authority of note clings to this early typographical error.

Now, to return to the purloined Golden Cowry, with just a little meander along the way to mention that there are also Golden Olives, but they are a mollusk of another color—or a different kettle of shellfish. The Golden Cowry is *Cypraea aurantium,* a distinct species, whereas a Golden Olive is a sport, a mutation, a freak if you will, within various species of *Olividae,* notably *O. incrassata* and *O. sayana.* A golden specimen of the latter is what collectors scramble for in Florida, if necessary over the prone bodies of their dearest friends.

The value of such hard-won prizes is difficult to determine, for how can you set a price on a four-leaf clover? I've heard rumors of hundreds, even thousands of dollars, but have yet to see a price tag or a listing of anything approaching those numbers. It may well be that buyers pledge sellers to secrecy so they can boast they found the specimens themselves.

My Golden Cowry was priced at $200, and it was absolutely gorgeous. It glowed like orange jade, and you could lose yourself in its depths. Everyone who came into the shop, including four-year-old children, wanted it more than anything else there, and wanted at least to hold it if they could not own it. They could not understand my reluctance to take it out of the case, and I would patiently explain that although I trusted them, each one of them individually, their attention might be diverted at the very moment I was called to the telephone and "someone else," some unscrupulous phantom prowler always looking for such lucky breaks, might take advantage of the situation.

The truth of the matter is that there are very few people I would trust with a Golden Cowry and a chance to make off with it. The darned things are hypnotic, compelling. A four-year-old might take it, not knowing it was worth more than a quarter, simply because it was pretty.

Some shells require a working knowledge of conchology to be appreciated, but not this one. It has its own built-in greatness. That is why, on South Sea Islands, it was always considered the property of the chief, and any diver who found one had to hand it over to the headman or risk fatal consequences. For years the only ones that came out of the islands were either smuggled out or proudly brought as the gift of a chief. The first Cowry I ever saw was one of a pair given to an American Naval doctor by the father of a grateful, and royal, patient during World War I. After the doctor's death, the sole heir decided that two Golden Cowries were a bit much and offered the smaller one for sale at $1000. He did not get that much, of

[65]

course, but it just shows how much he had been impressed by its value.

The second Cowry I saw was in the estate of a very old lady in Massachusetts, the daughter of a whaling captain. She had cut her teeth on the shell, and later used it as a darning egg. It was found among the needles and threads in her sewing basket. "Not worth anything moneywise," she probably thought, "but pretty, pretty enough to keep near forever." And it still was, when I saw it, even with its needle pricks and baby-teeth marks.

The one I had in the shop was fresh, live-taken by a native boy in the British Solomon Islands, and was both the joy of my life and the bane of my existence. Although I hated to see it go when I sold it to a friend, who gave me visiting privileges, it was a relief not to have it around.

I wasn't half so apprehensive when, a few weeks later, the same native boy in the Solomons sent me a *Conus gloria-maris,* the Glory-of-the-Sea Cone, which is the rare shell that has enjoyed the best relationship with the press throughout the ages. That was the one that had bee-lined me into the McArthur Shop in the first place.

Honestly, if I were another shell (which I sometimes, with delusions of grandeur, think I am), I'd be so mad at that stuck-up Gloria who is always getting her name in the papers every time she turns around! But I saw her get her comeuppance in my shop.

The sixty-first specimen of *C. gloria-maris* collected since record keeping began in 1757 simply lay there under a Victorian glass dome and the unknowing asked, "Why is that one under glass? Is there something special about it?" One person was even more insulting, offering me $50 for the dome and telling me not to bother to throw in the shell. A devout collector who was present at the time has never fully recovered from this display of heresy.

The truth is that I am myself a heretic in this instance. I adore the cone family, and always say that if it were decreed that I could personally collect only one genus I could make do with cones. After all, there are over four-hundred species of them, and the highest degree of variability within each species. I can't imagine cones ever becoming boring.

Queen Gloria is by no means my favorite. This isn't just sour grapes because I know I cannot afford her. She has a publicity-shy but rarer and more expensive cousin called *Conus milne-edwardsi,* the Glory of India, for which I would mortgage the shell shop—my equivalent for selling my soul to the Devil. India's Glory has that indescribable extra added something that makes you speak in a whisper and turns your resistance to putty. She would be worth whatever one had to pay to possess her, for one could delight in her intrinsic loveliness forever.

For my taste *gloria-maris* cannot make it on her own without her press agent, like a movie star whose sole claim to reverence is that she commands $1,000,000 per picture. I've seen understudies with more talent, and cheaper cones with more *je ne sais quoi.* If someone offered me one for $15 with the stipulation that I must keep her and not sell her for the enormous profit that the purchase price would represent, I would say thanks very much, but no thanks. I'd rather buy five $3 charmers.

My indifference was shared by the visitors to my shop unless they recognized the star or until I dropped her name and price. Then their eyes popped, and she began to look better to them. I kept her there for a month, even though she was bespoken the day she arrived. I wanted the regulars to have at least a glimpse of her, knowing they would reproach me if I denied them the chance, and figuring that if they stayed away for a whole month they would have forfeited their rights to be considered regulars.

Everyone I wanted to see her reported in. Word went out on the shell-collectors' grapevine, and I received letters from far-flung old-style collectors who needed a *gloria-maris* to complete their set. But no one who saw her swooned, offered me his right arm if I would double-cross the original buyer, nor lost any sleep because he could not have her, so far as I know. And I never knew a second's worry that some love-smitten stranger might steal her. To anyone I suspected might have ulterior motives, I always made it abundantly clear that a hot *gloria-maris* would be hard to unload.

Three days after her arrival, a man in Topeka, Kansas, had known her length to the millimetre, and the condition of her lip, the number of blemishes on her shoulder. He wrote asking me to give him second refusal should the first buyer change his mind. A world populated solely by people in a position and with a will to buy this shell is necessarily small, and an alert signal can circle it in a trice. No one would dare buy a shell even remotely resembling my *gloria* if she were stolen, unless he wanted just to gloat over her in private instead of showing her off. But what satisfaction would that be, if you couldn't let anyone in on the secret? If a buyer of stolen goods yielded to temptation and flashed her about, some blabbermouth might get him arrested as an accessory after the fact.

The most sensational heist of a *gloria-maris* ever pulled was the famous theft from the American Museum of Natural

SHE SELLS SEASHELLS

History circa 1950. I have often pondered the fate of this unfortunate specimen and the misguided individual who took it.

It was in a small case all by itself, separated from the other shells, with a card proclaiming it to be the most valuable in the world, worth, at that time, $1,500. "Yes, but to whom?" might well have been added, for unless the thief, after he had spirited case and all out of the Museum, knew precisely where to deliver it he was in for a disappointment. A shell isn't like the Hope Diamond which can be cut up into several gems and marketed profitably. It is like a Rembrandt that had been measured with calipers and documented to a fare-thee-well. Unless the thief had access to the limited list of potential buyers and knew for a fact that one of them was both acquisitive and insane enough to buy it, where would he turn? As far as I know, there are no fences who specialize in hot seashells, and anyone with a general line of stolen merchandise would think a shell stealer was mad. It is my educated guess that after a few razzings and several fruitless efforts, the frustrated thief tossed *gloria* out with the garbage.

The specimen now displayed at the Museum is a model, a dead ringer, so cleverly fabricated by artist and devoted shell collector Anthony D'Attilio that people who do not carefully read all the printed information in the case assume it to be real.

The one I sold, number Sixty-one, was real and is now a jewel in her owner's collection. In my shop the dome under which she once nestled now covers a *Harpa costata*, the Imperial Harp, priced at $40. *Sic transit gloria-maris.*

I might not have been so nonchalant throughout *gloria-maris'* sojourn in the shop had *McArthur's* shoplifters still been on the prowl. However, that tiny ring of shell thieves, as we discovered it to be, had not dared to show its collective nasty face near a shell shop in years. I am happy to say that I was present at the high noon of its downfall, and perhaps made a significant contribution to its undoing.

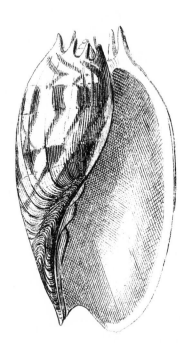

Nine

Jesse James, one of the two bandits besetting McArthur, was not as wild about shells as his friend, Billy the Kid. Billy had a fever for them, as some people have for emeralds. Many persons react this way, but Billy had the double-trouble of no self-control and insufficient funds. In his early twenties, he had had the sickness since childhood, always the craving for more and more shells which must somehow be satisfied. Nevertheless, I doubt if he would have gone to the lengths he did without the urging and collaboration of his brasher pal, Jesse.

I first saw Billy on the Wednesday of my second experimental week in the shop. He was sitting across the big desk from Braun, listening raptly to one of the old man's anecdotes.

I got the distinct impression that I was intruding upon some interminable, murmuring, pointless yet somehow ritualistic colloquy that had been going on for ages. I felt like an uncalled-for adult who had surprised two youthful smokers of corn silk behind a barn.

Billy uncoiled to his feet, and Braun introduced us. Billy was, to misquote Braun for the purpose of non-identification, a sculptor, just getting started now but so gifted that he would eventually be one of my better customers if I bought the place.

He was crazy about seashells. Suiting the stage business to the text, Billy went to one of the cabinets and opened a drawer. To his credit, I must say that he indulged in no little bleats designed to portray "the man crazy about seashells." He just looked at them, drawer after drawer. He must have seen everything in there at least a hundred times. I sensed something fishy about the performance.

(I have inner radar, if I may be forgiven such immodesty, which goes "ping" when something is wrong. I may be wrong about the character and degree of the wrongness, as I recently was in appraising the credit rating of a potential customer. Hearing a loud, clear ping, I refused to let him walk out with nearly $100 worth of merchandise until his check had cleared. I made an enemy for life, who slips vitriolic little notes under my door whenever he is in the vicinity. So I was wrong, but not entirely. No deadbeat he; actually he is the kind of big spender most shopkeepers pray for, but his subsequent actions nevertheless proved him to be a detestable human being, and I am happy not to have him underfoot.)

Billy wasn't detestable. You had to feel sorry for him. He reeked of failure—not just monetary failure, not just temporary financial embarrassment, but the permanent flaw of not ever being good enough at his chosen or any substitute calling. One of the things about my New York I most enjoy is the vital kids from all over who congregate here and many of whom gravitate toward my shop. The kids who have what it takes show it from the very beginning. There is a sparkle and drive about them that tells you if they take a fancy to seashells, it will be ten-cent Money Cowries today, Goldens tomorrow.

Billy's longings for Goldens and Glories-of-the-Sea stuck out like a sore, festering thumb. He seemed hurt and bewildered that the world had not thrust them upon him as he paid twenty-five cents and a penny tax for a *Natica hilaris*. Then, with a quavery small smile for Braun and a curt nod in my direction, he left, obviously as wary and unloving of me as I was of him.

Braun recorded this first, and final, sale of the day in his elegant script. That nice boy, he said, dropped by for a chat almost every week. Sometimes he did not even have a quarter for a shell, but he liked to look at them. The old man seemed enormously pleased and flattered that Billy also valued the chat.

Braun cut up Susie's pork liver with a rusty pair of shears and put the pie plate on the floor near her hideaway. He straightened his Homburg and bade me good afternoon.

It was a dark day outside and inside, since for reasons of economy only about fifty percent of the available lighting sources was ever utilized. Susie emerged to sniff at her food, then took her daily stiff-legged constitutional around the nautilus case then back under the radiator. The mood was gloomy. I sought solace in mathematics.

What kind of business man, eager to unload an unprofitable enterprise, would leave his chosen sucker alone for hours with the books? My cousin Crosbie McArthur, that's who. And what sucker, having had ample time in which to pore over the ugly facts, would buy? Guess.

Actually I did not have access to all the facts, since a segment of the evidence was missing from the tall slim ledger in which sales were listed. Braun's calligraphy was there, alternating with McArthur's more mundane scrawl, but there was not as much as a chicken scratch attributable to the third man, the mysterious Mister Doe. It was almost as though there were no such day as Saturday. I was sure that McArthur had these totals written down somewhere for income-tax purposes, but I would not stoop to snooping through his private papers. The ledger, I assured myself, was practically public property for all to read. The tale it told was dismal indeed, and whatever spice Doe might have supplied would have helped.

I had noticed the lack of Saturday entries the week before when I first began studying the records, but I didn't want to come right out and ask McArthur about it. If I exhibited too much interest in the book he might, recognizing its power to depress me and queer the deal, snatch it away before I was halfway through.

Fortunately, McArthur had still been in the store when I arrived on Monday. Taking over the ledger, I saw that the last entry bore the date of the preceding Friday. I seized the opportunity.

"What happened to Saturday?" I asked. "Didn't John Doe show up, or didn't the customers?"

"John never writes in the book."

"He doesn't?" As if I didn't know. "Why not?"

He told me. Doe's reason was, befitting the man, peculiar. It seems he did not want the income-tax people to know that he was moonlighting, earning, perhaps, the exact number of dollars that would nudge him into a higher bracket. As long as his handwriting did not appear in the book, the government could never prove that he had worked there. He kept track of his sales on loose slips of paper which were destroyed after the pertinent material was abstracted. For all I know, he may personally have swallowed them the following Saturday.

"He sold seventeen dollars worth this week," said McArthur. "No, wait. He sold seventeen dollars worth plus a dollar an hour for his wages—Twenty-five. He takes out his wages and puts the rest in an envelope which he hides some place we have agreed upon. Weeks when he doesn't take in enough to cover his wages he leaves me a U O Me."

"And you take his word for it?" I was shocked by this informal financial arrangement.

"Sure."

"Maybe you shouldn't. Maybe all those rare shells you thought had been stolen were actually sold on Saturdays, and Doe simply put the cash in his own pocket. How do you know he didn't destroy some of the slips he made out before you even saw them?"

My cousin pooh-poohed the idea and chided me for a devious imagination, which was the result, or cause, of having written mystery stories. After all, I did not know the man, and he did. He trusted him.

But I had put a bug in his ear, and he began to brood. The amazing coincidence of a series of thefts occuring only on Saturdays slowly made sense to him. Not my kind of sense. His version was that Doe was systematically stealing the shells to sell elsewhere or to enhance his own collection. By Friday he had worked himself up into such a lather that immediate action was required. He changed the locks, so the key in Doe's possession would do him no good when he showed up the next day to steal more. Then he telephoned me.

"Can you come in tomorrow?" he asked.

There was no reason why I couldn't, so I said, "Sure. But what happened to what's-his-name?"

"He's a crook. Nothing but a darned crook."

"You caught him? You found out that he had been selling shells and pocketing . . ."

"Nope. But I got to thinking about it and realized he's a crook." McArthur told me what he had done about the locks, adding, "Since you're coming in tomorrow, you don't have to come in this afternoon. Braun says he can stay. I'll leave the new key in the barber shop next door, and you can pick it up in the morning."

"Okay," I said blithely, hanging up. I could do the things today I had planned to put off until tomorrow.

Then I started to do a little realizing myself. I got the picture. Tomorrow morning a man would try to open the door of a shop, where he might earn a dishonest dollar, with a key that would not work. He would go to the corner saloon to drown his troubles. A man whose face I did not know would return later in the day, stewed to the gills. We would find me, the woman who had stolen his job, wrecked his life, and changed the locks on him. Even perfectly sober he might feel inclined to kill me.

I am not the type to be cast as heroine in a Gothic novel. I called McArthur back.

"We can't do it this way," I said. "You've got to think up some excuse—anything but the real one—about why you don't want him working there any longer, and you've got to be there in the morning to tell it to him. And don't, please, blame it on me. Don't let him think you are letting him go because I selfishly want to work Saturdays. It's your problem. It began a long time before I came back in, so I must insist that you handle it."

He got mad, of course, but he conceded me the point. Women! With their crazy imaginations!

McArthur could not think of a plausible lie, so he settled for a half-truth. He told Doe that I had already decided to buy the shop, and there was a relative who wanted to work Saturdays who would be putting up some of the money, so there was no use arguing. Doe took it philosophically and fished in his pocket for the key which was now excess baggage. He kept it on a ring with three others that opened doors in his other life. To be sure he was returning the right one, he tried them all in the door. None, of course, worked. McArthur told him I was the nervous type who had already demanded that the lock be changed so that unauthorized personnel could not come and go at will.

Doe asked if he could use the phone to call me and wish me all the success in the world. His opening remarks were effusively in that vein; then he went on to say that I probably would not succeed if I had such a low opinion of my fellow human beings that I expected the worst of them; hate was reflected in hate and he would pray for me. I thanked him and asked him to put McArthur on the phone.

"Get rid of him," I said. "Tell him to go do his praying somewhere else. I'm going downtown now, but I'll wait across the street until the awning is up. Put it up the minute he leaves."

"It's up now," McArthur said.

"Then put it down when he leaves."

"Okay."

McArthur was sitting on a camp chair outside the shop when I rounded the corner. The awning was up so he could enjoy the morning sun. He caught sight of me and beckoned. I guessed that the coast was clear.

Doe was indeed gone, but his melody lingered on throughout the day to plague me. I, who used to be Queen of Saturday adored by my loyal subjects, was treated like the leader of an unpopular coup d'état. The Saturday regulars, and there were quite a few of them, started coming in around noon. Every one asked where the "nice man" was. "He had such a lovely smile."

One of the regulars, well-known to his cronies, was Billy the Kid. This surprised me no end. Braun, never one to leave even the most trivial detail out of a story, had told me that Billy came in religiously once a week to see him and the shells, but had notably not mentioned that he also favored Doe with periodic visits. I figured that Billy, for reasons of his own, had kept his weekend infidelity a secret. Braun would be happier thinking he was Billy's one and only favorite shell seller. Tactful consideration for the old man's vanity might have made Billy reticent, but I wondered if he did not have another motive.

Billy looked different on Saturday. He was less humble. He stood taller, straighter, and walked proudly instead of shuffling. He smiled instead of seeming about to cry.

With him was a laugher, his pal Jesse James. Jesse looked like a youthful Mephistopheles, dark, with a widow's peak on either side of which I could easily imagine budding horns, satanic eyebrows, laughing eyes and lips. I did not doubt that what would make him laugh most would be cruel, outrageous, even illegal. My radar, which had pinged for Billy, bonged for Jesse. I congratulated myself for having made two changes in the shop first thing that morning.

Cousin Crosbie had always displayed a tray of volutes, including some of his most expensive items, in the far end of the showcase. This made them readily liftable by even the most inept shoplifter since he would only have to push a sliding back-panel, bend his elbow, reach in, and grab something worth the effort without even looking. Volutes are smooth and easy to palm. I had transposed their tray with one containing several species of spiny, bristling *Murex* well-equipped to fight off an intruder as well as to become so entangled with each other that a blind effort to extract one would end in a shambles, and possibly bloodshed.

My other change involved the cash box. The way McArthur had set it up a thief would have been able to unsnarl *Murices* at his own chosen speed. The box was in a drawer in the farthest west corner of the shop, behind a partition which cut off the view of what went on up front. The light was bad back there, and change making was a slow process. If a culprit had the forethought to pay for twenty cents worth of shells, plus a penny tax, with a $10 bill, he could select something choicer at his leisure. I had moved the box to a drawer immediately behind the partition, from which point I could see and could be disconcertingly seen by all present.

It took some doing but I never removed my eyes from Billy and Jesse all the while they were there. Perhaps I was just being sensitive, but I felt they did not like me one bit better than I liked them and that they, more than anyone else,

[79]

resented my being there instead of sweet old John Doe. I thought Jesse's eyebrows angled more sharply when he beheld *Murex* where *Voluta* ought to be, and I am sure he muttered something derogatory under his breath as I stood, foursquare, watching him as I made change.

When they took their paltry little purchase and waved bye-bye to me from the open door, I could at last relax. I went to the back of the shop to get water for coffee. I drank it zestfully, thinking "what a smart girl am I." Clearly, I had outmaneuvered them, for every shell in sight was still where it had been at their entrance, minus the two little *Naticas* for which they had paid.

My smugness was soon deflated by the appearance of other members of John Doe's Fan Club, but I managed to make it to closing without bursting into tears. At the last stroke of five I locked the door from the inside and performed the nightly task of totaling up the day's receipts, emptying the ashtrays, hiding the money, etc., etc. (Note to future thieves: we don't hide money in the shop any more. We have a new system. We hide it in a bank.) Then I got my coat and bonnet, turned off all but the one light which should be left burning, and tried to unlock the door.

Perhaps I'd better explain about that last chore, although it is difficult to explain something you don't quite understand yourself. You could not lock the door to the shop from the inside by turning a knob, as I did in my apartment, nor did it then have a slide bolt of the kind I have since installed. You had to use a key, but not the same one from the inside out as you used from the outside in. It was a special key that hung on a nail amidshop. These complications had something to do with the fact that McArthur, ever a do-it-yourselfer, frequently changed the lock for one reason or another. To save time and money he changed the outside lock only. The inside lock had gracefully adjusted itself to several new partners, but with this latest one it was wholly incompatible. The key refused to budge and broke in two when I tried to force it. No two ways about it, I was locked in. Instantly I panicked.

I could call the cops, or the Fire Department. There was usually an emergency key kept in the barber shop next door, I remembered, but I was not at all sure that McArthur had thought to or had time to have a duplicate of the new one made to leave there. When you are desperate you'll reach for any straw, so I decided to phone the barber and find out. I got the classified telephone directory.

I could not think of the barber's name.

Should I scan the columns for the address nearest me? I did not have my reading glasses with me, the numbers were fuzzy and indistinct, and there are an awful lot of places in New York where a fellow can get his hair cut.

I started thinking about the police and firemen again, but I knew that would mean breaking the door down and leaving the place open to looters over the balance of the weekend. I would have to call McArthur in Westchester first to get his permission for such a step. I knew *his* number, but before dialing it I went to the door, pressed my nose against its glass, and looked out longingly.

Nothing has ever more delighted me than that sight of a neighbor's child walking her puppy. I rapped on the glass, caught her eye and tried to explain in dumb show what I needed. She was a bright girl, but of course she couldn't understand. What sort of idiot gets herself locked in? But at last I managed to wigwag and mouth instructions to tell her to get what's-his-name, the barber. She did so.

I made key-turning motions to him. He nodded and smiled and went to fetch it. It wouldn't work. It was a duplicate of the old one.

I sought, and, fortunately, found inner calm. There was, I recalled, a mail-slot in the door. I took the new key out of my purse and slipped it through. What's-his-name picked it up and put it in the lock. It worked! For all I understand about locks it might not have, if the antagonism between it and the inside lock were mutual. If it had not worked, I believe I would have gone clear off my rocker.

I barely glanced in the show window as I relocked the door behind me, but I vaguely sensed that there was something odd about it. There was a space. There never was a space in a McArthur window because his style of window-dressing was "show them everything you have." It always looked like a pushcart, but tonight there was a puddle of nothing spang in the middle. I supposed that Braun had sold a large piece of coral or a clam or something on Friday and forgotten to replace it.

That my supposition was far off target I learned Monday morning when an agitated McArthur called to ask if I had sold the big *Voluta mammilla,* worth $50, that had been in the window.

"No, I didn't," I said.

"Well, it's gone. Somebody must have swiped it."

I could not believe it, and I was just plain scared. Had the curse upon Saturdays retained its power despite all my efforts at exorcism?

[82]

"When did you last see it?" I asked feebly. "I mean, couldn't it have been taken another time?"

"I think I would have noticed. I noticed this morning that it wasn't there."

"Have you asked Braun about it?" This was a wild hope. Braun sometimes took a busman's holiday on Sunday and went in to redo the window, which always ended up looking as frumpy as ever. He might have decided to put this particular shell somewhere else. Then I remembered the nothing-puddle, which altered the time factor. "Maybe he sold it the last thing Friday and didn't write it down," I said.

This was a possibility. Fred Braun rigidly observed the strictures against transacting business on the Sabbath, but if trapped in the shop a minute beyond sundown, he would graciously conclude any work in progress and hold the recording of it over until Monday. McArthur said he would ask him when he came in, then recalled that this was the day Braun was not coming in but was going to his dentist in New Jersey. Could I please come a little bit early to relieve him?

I could, indeed. I was eager to revisit the scene of the crime where I might better reconstruct its enactment. I could not buy my own feeble hope that Braun had made an extraordinary $50 sale at the precise moment when the sun sank slowly into the Hudson on Friday afternoon. That would be stretching the long arm of coincidence too far. It seemed obvious that the long arm of *something* had stretched into that window and seized the shell while I was there. My pride was crushed, and I could have cried my eagle eyes out.

Then I consoled myself with the thought that I had been up against professional thieves and that honest, simple folk rarely come out ahead in such an encounter. The Saturday thieves had been perfecting their technique over a long period of time. I was a novice adversary. However, I was sufficiently experienced to know that such characters usually operate as trios, thus outnumbering the most wily watcher's two eyes. Their winning tactic is a triple play, like Tinker to Evers to Chance. I had pegged Billy the Kid and Jesse James as Messrs. Tinker and Evers, but had given no thought to Chance.

Which one of those unfamiliar faces had been his? I had read and written enough mystery stories to know it would belong to the least likely. I tried to gather up the threads so I might reweave the plot. Who else had been in there while every speck of my attention was concentrated on Billy and Jesse?

There was an unobtrusive, undistinguishable little man fussing around with the seafans. He seemed the least likely one, and therefore a prime suspect. For all I knew he might have been John Doe himself. That would make sense. I had read, and written, worse plots than that. On previous Saturdays, Doe might have worked in cahoots with Billy and Jesse against McArthur, distracting other customers while the boys took what they wanted. Billy would already have decided what to take. During his weekly chat with Braun, that kindly dupe and unwitting fingerman would obligingly have pointed out what was new and choice and not cheap. The big volute in the window was scheduled to be the next acquisition but suddenly the signals, and locks, were changed, necessitating a new plan of action.

Doe (surely that unobtrusive little man was he—I distinctly recalled that he had a nice smile, which was the feature of my predecessor that everyone had mentioned) had phoned his cronies that the jig was up, that a female ogre had taken his

[84]

place behind the counter. Not to be denied their prize, determined to outwit me, the boys decided to overpower me by sheer, brute charm while their invisible partner strolled off with the loot toward the point of rendezvous.

It was a good plot, but it wouldn't hold water because one fact kept getting in the way. After making a mess of the pile of seafans, that man had walked out of the shop empty-handed. I remembered his taking one last look in the window from outside as he relit his pipe. Sure, I know that is the kind of flamboyant no-hands gesture a super-thief would make, but there wasn't a spot on this small man's person where he could have concealed a *Voluta mammilla*.

V. mammilla resembles exactly what you would expect it to upon hearing its name. This was a particularly robust one, over eleven inches in length. It was the sort of thing that would appeal to a sick-minded person who might be prompted to filch it not because of the money it was worth but for the mental images it evoked.

I was off on a tangent. In that context, perhaps Billy and Jesse had had nothing whatsoever to do with this particular crime. There were many psychiatrists in the vicinity. Perhaps a patient of one of them had at last given in to a long-time lust for this mammillary symbol. I had no idea how long it had been in the window, which I never looked at on purpose and saw only when it swung into my line of vision as I locked and unlocked the door.

The wedge-shaped window is as accessible as a smörgås-bord table, and people can easily help themselves. I dress it now with a variety of batik-like fabrics. Actually these are skirts from old dresses of mine which I never had the heart to throw away; I often say I had to buy the store just to find a use

[85]

for them. I strew them tastefully with shells keyed to their dominant colors, but I never include anything worth more than a couple of dollars, so that if temptation becomes irresistible I don't lose too much. Why tempt Fate with a $50 item?

Whoever stole the *Voluta* need not have feared being observed by someone looking in the window. He, or she (for there are also sick women), would simply have to stand with his back to me, contemplating the shell as though considering whether to buy it, until the passer-by moved on. But in order to turn, open the door, and make his exit, he would have had to conceal the shell or risk being seen by me. This meant that with forethought the thief had brought a portable hiding place, probably a shopping bag.

Who had carried shopping bags that fatal Saturday? Who hadn't? The only visitor I was positive did not have one was the alleged John Doe, whom I now reluctantly had to discharge for lack of evidence. All the others had carried some sort of tote bag in which they could stash the goods. The apparition had carried, of all things, a market basket.

The apparition. I had forgotten it, perhaps because it had not come wholly into my consciousness on that nervous day, just as it had not come wholly into the shop. Alone there now, I stared at the spot where it had materialized and tried to reconjure it. It had frightened me then, and it still did. It was huge, over six-feet high and two-feet broad, and it was dressed as a woman, wearing a black kerchief over its head, a shawl over its full-skirted black dress. It was the witch straight out of Snow White. Dark eyes, deeply set in a chalky face, caught mine. I thought it was going to ask a question, propound a riddle, and I fervently wished it would not, as I preferred to have nothing to do with it. It looked quite mad, but the not-for-realness about it disturbed me most. I felt it was pretending, play-acting, and was actually a very small bit of ectoplasm which had blown itself up out of all proportion. Heavy though it seemed, it had that floating quality of ectoplasm or of a badly laid-out corpse in a coffin.

To my relief, it merely pawed over the jewelry near the door—and, incidentally, near the window—with its enormous paws. I did not encourage it by a smile or a nod to come nearer. I turned to answer a question of Jesse's, and when I looked back, it was fleeing, black skirt a-flying. In all that yardage it could have concealed a dozen *V. mammillas,* but it had probably slipped the shell into the market basket, alongside the poisoned apple it would have offered me had I been more receptive.

Was it, perchance, Mr. Chance? Quite possibly. Billy Tinker and Jesse Evers were just the type who would number among their acquaintances a wag who adored wearing old theatrical costumes. They would be bosom buddies.

How could I tell those innocents, the Messrs. McArthur and Braun, that the world was currently a place in which such happenings happened? Especially, how could I tell Braun that the youth who worshipfully sat at his feet on weekdays was a changeling so complex that I was able to concoct this incredible story about him, and believe it wholly?

The story is still unverified. We know the facts about Billy and Jesse, and they are just as I surmised them. I have never again seen the apparition so as to be able to identify it positively, although one day, a month or so later, an enormous man came into the shop, looked around and left abruptly, leaving a space on top of a cabinet where a gorgeous black

Murex had been. In or out of skirts he may have been an independent operator, not part of the trio. Nevertheless, someone wisked the *Voluta* out of the window that day, when I'd swear it could not have been done. Impossible deeds are done in impossible ways, and the idea of a female impersonator stealing a *V. mammilla* is too magnificently surrealistic to be discarded. I shall always believe that this is what happened.

But how could I tell Braun as much of it as I felt he was old enough to hear? I would do it slowly and in person, I decided, breaking it to him gently that he had collaborated with a rascal who had done his employer out of hundreds of dollars and that he would have to learn not to trust every likely lad or lassie in the future.

When McArthur called in the evening to check on the day, I simply told him I was convinced I knew who was doing the stealing, who would bear watching. I said I would formulate my thoughts on the matter and reveal them Wednesday. I forgot to warn him not to tell anyone that Dick Tracy was ready to blow the lid off. I thought of that on the way down Wednesday, and the first thing I asked was whether they had mentioned it to anyone. No, said McArthur. No, said Braun; no one, that is, except his friend Billy, who had stopped in to see him Tuesday afternoon.

Ten

"He's the very person you should not have told," I said, and then went on to explain, too exasperated by Braun's pigheaded misjudgment of the boy to spare his feelings.

He was shocked, disposed not to believe any of it until I asked if he did not find it odd that Billy had never once mentioned coming in on Saturdays.

"Did he mention it yesterday?" I hammered away.

"No. No, he didn't. I told him the volute had disappeared on Saturday, and he didn't say it was here when he was, or that it wasn't. He just listened when I said that you were here instead of Doe, and he didn't say, 'I know she was.' You're right. It's odd, very odd."

"That it is. Let's look at the bright side. I don't think he has a very good opinion of me so he would not expect me to be able to see through anyone as clever as he. Let's leave it that way, give him enough rope to hang himself. That way we may be able to get back some of the loot."

"I won't let him inside the store," Braun said fiercely. "I will refuse to speak to him."

"That will ruin everything. Keep it as much like old times as you can, but be vigilant."

"It was flattering to an old man," he sighed ruefully, "to have a young one listen to him so attentively. All the time he was making a fool of me."

"You're an interesting old man," I assured him. "You'll find other and better youngsters to listen."

I made him promise to tell Billy that I suspected a tall woman of having taken the shell, one so unique in appearance that I would certainly recognize her if I ever saw her again. That would give Billy and Jesse a good, raucous laugh at my expense. I did not, of course, reveal my further suspicions about the woman to Braun, being afraid he might leak it.

Billy and Jesse, together or singly, continued to visit the shop as before. Billy was always his Saturday-self with me, charming and relaxed as though we were great pals. I let him think so. Nothing more was stolen. In fact, after I took over the shop, Billy bought two expensive shells from me, instead of his usual budget items. I felt that my mission had been accomplished, that he had reconciled himself to paying cash because he knew he would never catch me nodding.

He even said that he had plenty of spare time and would be glad to help me out in the store if I needed him. I laughed up my sleeve as I wrote down his address and phone number.

SHE SELLS SEASHELLS

That would be the day! But on the surface our relationship was so good that he even tried to sell me shells.

He brought in four cones, fairly rare ones. I said I really didn't want to buy anything of that sort then, what with all the expenses of remodeling and the need to buy commoner shells which would supply my bread and butter. He said I could have them at a bargain. I asked him to write down their names and the prices he would want, saying I would think about it and let him know. I was sure I was being invited to buy back some of the things stolen from McArthur which properly should have been part of my starting inventory.

At that time there were four other places in New York City selling seashells, although none with such singleness of purpose as my establishment. They also carried coins, or stamps, or gadgets on which to mount shells, and with so much else going on it would have been easy for them to lose a few specimens without noticing. I knew the proprietors of each place personally, and called them the next morning.

The unanimity of their responses was amazing. All had been visited by a pair of young men who seemed to know a lot about shells and who took a very long time selecting two or three inexpensive specimens. Shortly thereafter, something expensive had turned up missing. I did not put these words into their mouths. They volunteered the information. Clearly Billy and Jesse had been playing the field.

It would be bad enough to buy shells that rightfully belonged to me, but it would be even worse to become a receiver of stolen property. I read off to the proprietors the list of cones to learn if any were among the missing. None of Billy's offerings rang any bells, but the concerned parties promised to check their records. We would band together in an informal sort of Shell-Dealers' Protective Association, keeping each other informed as to the doings of the dreadful duo.

Apparently, in those other shops, the two had managed to blend into the background, looking, no matter how many times they were seen, like any other two young men out for an afternoon's browsing. Braun, after all, had proven to be their nemesis since he had given me a name for Billy, enabling me to pick him out of the crowd when I heard his friend address him. I might have taken the Saturday Billy to be a better adjusted double of the wistful weekday visitor, had the name, added to the resemblance, not provided positive identification.

There is a moral in here for shell lovers: it is all very well to love shells superficially, but they will mean so much more if you can put a name to them. Names make them come alive and will enable you to see them better.

There are also rules here for shoplifters, one of which would be never to exercise both sides of your dual personality in a single shop. Time schedules and personnel can be changed and ruin your act.

Within a week, another shopkeeper saw Billy adding four volutes to his collection without paying for them. He said nothing at the time, but later sent a bill to the name and address I had provided. Billy lashed back with a letter, indignant and wholly truthful, saying that he had not bought those shells and therefore had no intention of paying for them. The matter was not further pursued. It did not need to be. Billy and Jesse put two and two together and knew that their names were on a conchological wanted-poster and that a posse was after them. They have nevermore been seen inside a shell shop.

That is the only practical way these thefts can be handled.

SHE SELLS SEASHELLS

Can you imagine trying to convince a police force that a man must be hunted down for having stolen a seashell? That said shell was worth a lot of money? That said stolen article could be so positively identified as to become exhibit A in an airtight case? Forget it.

No. The only thing we dealers can do is to keep a file of known criminals and cut the poor addict off from his source of supply. I bet Billy often wishes he had been a good boy, and I frequently feel sorry for him.

I was most grateful not to have him underfoot, however, during those early days of shop-owning, for I had quite enough with which to contend: electricians; painters; floor-layers; suppliers who had never heard of me and could not be expected to take me on faith; customers who knew more than I did. Still, it was euphoric, like the honeymoon of a bride who suspects in her lucid moments that she has married a monster.

Married we were, the shop and I, for better or worse. My attorney and McArthur's accountant had tied the knot on the afternoon of Friday, May twenty-fourth, nineteen-hundred-and-sixty-four, in the presence of another vitally interested party, the landlord.

Florence Belsky, my attorney, who sometimes acts as if she is my mother—or everybody's mother—disapproved of the match. She had not even known I was going steady when I called her the week before and broke it to her cold.

"Florence," I said, "I've bought a seashell store and I want you to draw up the papers."

"You've *what?*" she shot back.

"I've bought a seashell store," I repeated nonchalantly, as if to say, "doesn't everyone?"

"What do you mean you 'bought' it? How could you buy it

without consulting me? That's what I'm here for. I could have looked into it to find out if it's a sound proposition."

"I know." (That's why I had avoided telling her, because I had looked into it and knew it was about as unsound as a proposition could be. Positively flabby.)

"What kind of store did you say it was?"

"It sells seashells."

"Seashells! That's the most ridiculous thing I ever heard of. Aren't they those things you cut your feet on at the beach?"

"Yes, but they are also a whole lot more," I protested. "Just wait 'til you see them."

"You wait 'til I see them and have a look at the books and the lease and a few other things before you do anything rash. How far have you gone already?"

"All the way," I admitted. I could not possibly turn back. I was committed, and it was quite clear that Florence thought I should be.

She changed her mind a little bit when she saw what shells are really like, and has now been completely won over. She likes to quote Fiorello La Guardia to the effect that when she "makes a mistake it's a beaut," and she shudders when she thinks she might have talked me out of this happy union.

Nothing she could have said would have made the slightest impression on me for I was too far gone. Like a woman who wants to marry a reprobate because she feels that she, and she alone, can save him, I was deaf to good advice. There was no exact moment of decision. I gradually came to realize I was needed if the shop was ever to become what it could be. There was no time to be lost. It was like watching a sick person taking the wrong pills and sitting in drafts, and not lifting a finger to give him tender loving care.

[94]

SHE SELLS SEASHELLS

I tried to gain time by only half-buying the place, asking McArthur to stay on as a partner. The money I put in could be used to spruce it up and to stock it more attractively. But he wanted completely out. It had to be all or nothing. The partnership would never have worked. Every improvement I suggested he took as a criticism of his methods, which, of course, it was. He still refused to set an asking price, leaving the negotiations strictly to me.

Except for the missing Saturday figures, I knew to the penny how much the shop had earned over the past two years. It was my uneducated guess that when one bought a business one bought its income, not its inventory. I felt the price should be what one could reasonably expect to gross during the first year. Figuring on that basis, I came up with a sum so low I would have been embarrassed to offer it. So I upped it a little, shaving it as close as I dared because I would have whopping additional expenses in that first year, and I did not want to go broke before the end of it. There would be repairs, rent plus two months security, electricity, phone, and so forth. Meticulously I tried to forecast these and balance the whole against my available capital.

Parenthetically, I left out the most important item in the budget. Sharing the popular fallacy that seashells, at the source, are practically free, I had neglected to project what I would have to pay for merchandise. Blatantly shameless consultation of McArthur's books had made this seem a negligible expense. I had seen entries of a $500 payment to this supplier, $200 to that one, and assumed this to represent veritable mountains of seashells instead of the tiny windrows they later proved to be. I am probably the only person who ever bought a shop without first checking wholesale price lists.

I had overlooked the obvious fact that the present owner bought few shells because he sold few. It was my firm intent to sell more, as well as to maintain the best-stocked shop of its kind in the world. It would not be "Seashells Unlimited" in name only, if I had anything to say about it. It did not occur to me that this would cost money. And a good thing, too, or I would have lost my nerve completely.

I bearded McArthur with my paltry offer, and he snapped at it. In his weary and restless mood I think he would have accepted an even lower one. I have since been told by those in the know that I was a trifle generous; I could have got the shop for peanuts because there was no one with experience in the field who would have outbid me. Barring the miraculous appearance of someone who knew absolutely nothing about seashells but thought it might be profitable to sell them, he would have had to pack up his shells and go home, closing the shop forever. That is what I was afraid would happen, and it would have broken my heart.

So I surrendered.

Eleven

Even though the shop legally became mine shortly after three o'clock that Friday afternoon, I quixotically told the now retired McArthur that I thought the day's take belonged to him, instead of mincing it up into A.M. and P.M. sales, which might complicate future bookkeeping. He did not argue with me.

It was a lovely day for a wedding, bright and mild; and I did rather good business when the guests and officials had departed, better than had been done all week. I took this to be a good omen.

I am a firm believer in omens. It was therefore upsetting that Saturday turned out to be cold and drizzly, with a very long pause between customers. After all, Friday had belonged to McArthur; Saturday was the first day that was all my own, and it was behaving horribly. The gods, I felt, might be angry, although I had done everything I could think of to propitiate them.

A man I shall always adore, even though he seems successfully to have kicked the seashell habit, came in at about eleven o'clock. It was then that I decided the shop did not have to open earlier than that, and so it has been ever since. The hours before that can be killers that chill you to the bone. Besides, people who haven't the patience to wait until eleven o'clock to buy seashells don't deserve to have them.

Customer number one was a part-time opera singer whose far less glamorous full-time occupation enabled him to indulge his passion for cones. So dearly did he love the genus *Conus* that he sang for joy when he beheld them. I thought, "I did it and I'm glad." I might rue my rashness later, but how else would I have been able to hear snatches of arias sung in a mellifluous baritone in my very own shop, in praise of my very own merchandise? There are, I keep telling myself, more important things than money.

He bought $18 worth and asked for many cones I did not have. I wrote down the names and promised to get them all for him as soon as I found out who might be in a position to sell them to me.

When he left I returned to the task I had begun on arrival, that of removing everything from the hated window and finding some place to stash it. Millions, or so it seemed, of dirty little boxes containing dirty little shells were lumped together like so many nuts and bolts.

SHE SELLS SEASHELLS

It was such fun to do my first window that time ran by swiftly. It was past two o'clock before I noticed I was hungry and sat down behind the desk to eat lunch. I loathed that desk almost as much as the window, and I decided that if the Salvation Army would not accept it as a gift I would gladly pay someone to chop it up for firewood. It ate up far too much space in the tiny shop, and all of the drawers stuck.

It had its uses, though, I discovered after I got rid of it. A young mother breezed in one day carrying her baby in a wicker basket which she all but set down upon the desk that wasn't there. I stopped her from what had obviously been a habit just in the nick of time.

I had just finished my lunch when an extremely good-looking young man poked his head in the door and asked if a tall red-headed girl had come in yet. It wasn't hard to recall that she had not, for I had entertained no living creature since the baritone.

"That's funny," he said. "We're to meet here. I walked down from Seventy-fifth Street and she took a bus. I wonder what that crazy kid is up to."

"You're welcome to wait," I said. "It's raining pretty hard and you must be soaked."

"I'm hungry. When she comes in, tell her I'm having lunch in the chili place across the street. Can I bring you anything?"

"No, thanks. I've just eaten."

He loped across the street, looking like something absolutely gorgeous out of an Italian movie. I later learned that he was a Hollander.

Suddenly, nothing happened. No short blondes, medium brunettes, nor tall redheads appeared on the scene. I was accursed. The gods were mad at me, for sure. Then she showed up, a tall red-haired goddess whom he had neglected to say was as beautiful as he.

I gave her the message, but she did not have time for food, or the gentleman. She was absolutely insane about seashells and had never before been turned loose among so many. I let her have the run of the place, allowing her to look through all the cabinets and reserve stock. She had perfect taste, as some people have perfect pitch, and she pounced with a yelp of glee on every one of the better specimens McArthur had left me. She placed these on the desk, pending her final selection, and that great acreage of wood was soon as cluttered as the window used to be.

It was the first time she had ever been anywhere where seashells were sold, and she reacted like a kid in a candy store. Her only previous collecting had been in the Red Sea. Her last job had taken her to Elath, Israel, where she spent every available minute in the Sea, swimming, snorkling, and, after the first *Cypraea pantherina* had winked at her, shelling.

Actually, cowries wink in reverse. Other pursuers of these shells have told me of revisiting areas where they had formerly found them abundant only to find the place apparently deserted. Lingering for one last hopeful moment they were delighted to find that there had been no mass evacuation; slowly, one snail after another withdrew its mantle, and the shells twinkled like stars coming out on a summer night.

Lois, my new customer, had found not only cowries but had bagged practically every species known to be in that region, including what might well set a world's record for Textile Cones, which, according to her shellfish story, measured a good ten inches, although the maximum is supposed to be about six inches. I am sorry to say that shell fishermen are quite as prone to exaggeration as their piscatorial counterparts, and you really should hear their tales of the ones that got away. Talk about Loch Ness monsters!

I gasped when she spoke of this particular find. Was she aware, I asked, that *Conus textile* could have stung her to death? Not at the time, she said. Later, someone told her about the venom sack and the harpoon-like stinger with which this species and others of its genus defend themselves and incapacitate their prey.

Cones are carnivorous, in contrast to the vegetarian *Tridacna gigas,* libelously called "the Man-Eating Giant Clam." No *T. gigas* worth his salt would ever have to cheat on his diet and partake of man-meat because his larder was empty. These clams are efficient farmers, growing their own algae in the folds of their fleshy mantles, providing themselves with strategically placed transparent cells through which light can penetrate and stimulate growth even deep within the interior.

Although not indulging in the game of man-eating, they have had the name firmly fixed upon them. They are also called "Killer Clams." Who has not read a news item emanating from the Indo-Pacific region reporting the tragic death of a diver who ran afoul a Killer Clam? The alleged victim is always said to have been innocently swimming by when his foot was caught between the enormous valves, which immediately clamped shut upon it. ("Clamp," according to *Webster's Unabridged,* is an obsolete word for "clam." Think that over.) The reliable journalist who attempts to check the facts of one of these stories always reaches a dead end. He may find a friend of a friend, or a relative of a relative of someone who witnessed the killing, but the actual eyewitness is forever elusive. Obviously, to an ex-mystery-writer, the eyewitness is on the lam because he dunnit—because he murdered his co-worker in cold blood for a sack of pearls, then pinned the rap on a mollusk.

Give a clam a bad name and you might as well hang him. Even Clarence Darrow could not persuade a jury to acquit him. I defend *T. gigas* on the grounds that he would not touch meat and am told that this is nit-picking. What does it matter whether he kills by consumption or by drowning? He may prefer a rutabaga to a mouthful of diver's foot, but once he has clamped, can he unclamp quickly enough to do the man any good? Even if he can, would not the man have been so severely gashed by the sharp edges of the valves as to be unable to swim to the surface? I explain that when the clam is alive those "sharp" edges are covered with a cushy material like the rubber bumpers of subway doors. In addition many clams exist completely encased in coral, as though in a block of cement, and are therefore unable to open and shut at all. I show them color slides of living *T. gigas* to prove to them that the mantle stretches solidly, except for two small openings, from valve to valve. I point out that a diver would have to be suicidal to shove his foot far enough inside for him to become trapped. But it's no use. The defense gets clobbered every time, and the guilty go free.

Not so with our friends the cones. There are numerous accredited records of fatal poisonings and cases in which only prompt and skillful medication has saved lives. Members of our Armed Forces stationed in the Pacific are given a list of five cones they must treat with respect. Top billing goes to *Conus geographus,* a pinkish mauve gem covered with brown blotches shaped like imaginary countries on a geographical map. Beware also of the cones, *striatus, imperialis, marmoreus,* and *textile,* but if you really want my advice don't wait to be introduced and be wary of them all. Many cones are covered by a periostracum, an outer skin, which may make on-the-spot identification difficult. So I would take no chances in an area where poisonous species abide. The experienced cone collector seizes his prize by the shoulder, hopefully at the point furthest away from the aperture. He holds the specimen out of water until it dies before placing it in his collecting bag or the pocket of his diving suit. Many a cone has used its radula, which is a sort of many-toothed tongue, to chew through fabric, enabling it to sting its captor during the swim back to shore.

Lois knew none of this as she idled off Elath. Perhaps it was just dumb luck that she suffered no dire consequences, or maybe her whopper (in either sense of the word) had lived so long that all the sting had gone out of him. I tend toward the luck theory. Every day, hurrying toward the strip of beach she liked the best, she passed a group of workmen who invariably yelled at her, grimaced, and waved their arms. Lois, who could not speak Hebrew, assumed they were saying that she was trespassing on private property. Since they did not physically stop her nor seem inclined to press the matter further, she went on her merry way. She found out later that what they had been trying to tell her was that this particular cove was notorious for the ferocity, and preponderance, of its man-eating sharks. Only an idiot would choose to swim there. Clearly, she led a charmed life.

Lois did not give a thought to the danger, only to the wonder. Whatever marvels she saw, there was always a seductive reef dead ahead, promising more. She would lose track of outgoing mileage, so the incoming trips were always longer than she expected, the last few strokes being almost more than she could make. By the next day, however, she would have forgotten the aching arms, the weary body, and be all set for another go.

Her present job kept her in Montreal where the swimming was nothing to brag about. She "worked for the World's Fair." She had been "sent down to New York this weekend to see it."

That is what I understood her to say, but of course I wasn't too alert mentally at the time. I had been through a lot. It isn't every week you buy a store. You don't put all the money you should save for your old age into a pile and hand it over for something you may some day wish you had never seen, something you may not be able to manage. I felt I was in even more dangerous waters than those off Elath. End of excuse.

I thought that the powers that be out at Flushing, where our Fair had opened a couple of weeks earlier, had hired attractive young women to promote their product in various key cities. Lois, I figured, was the ballyhoo agent in Montreal, sent here to gather material for her sales talk.

Within that frame of reference she was neglecting her job, not to mention everything else but seashells. The handsome young man returned in search of her, and she barely said hello to him. He urged her to take a break and eat a little something. She said she wasn't hungry. He nagged her gently, but evidently he knew her well enough to sense the futility, and admitted he was licked. (The reason some people don't like seashells is that they once were fond of someone who liked them too much.) He said he'd mosey up to Sam Goody's shop to listen to records and then come back for her.

She was limiting herself to shells costing under $5 each, except for a purple *Chlamys nobilis* (Noble Scallop) that she could not resist even though it cost twice that much. I began to wonder, however, just how good Lois was at arithmetic, and whether she realized that multiples of $5, even of quarters, have a tendency to mount up to a sizeable figure. Concurrently, with a thrill, I knew that if she bought as much as half of what she had selected I would indeed be in business. My attorney, my accountant, and all those other sourpusses would just have to admit they'd been wrong.

As it turned out, she couldn't resist almost all of them. The invoice became a mess as I kept crossing out items and then putting them back in when she decided she could not live without them. She reminded me of a friend of mine who constantly complained because she had too many cats around her home; at one point the census stood at twenty-eight. As each new litter was expected my friend would vow to give all the kittens away and would line up a serious group of adoptive parents. The trouble was that there was never a specific kitten with which she could part.

"You can't have *that* one," she'd say indignantly, "it has white paws." Or it was all white, or all black, or striped, or it had two eyes, four legs, and a tail. Any trumped-up reason would do, and the would-be parents went away empty-handed.

Similarly, Lois would find some flimsy reason for not returning a shell to stock. It was too pink, too large, too small, too symmetrical, too *something,* and, besides, it spoke to her.

Her bill amounted to $142, plus tax. She asked if she could pay me by check and I said yes, if she had identification. I felt a twinge because I would much have preferred cash. Not that I didn't trust her. I had been with her for hours, and by now I loved her. But everything that was appealing about her was poetic, not practical. A girl as extravagant as this, as wholehoggish, might very well be chronically overdrawn at the bank. Moreover, what had she been up to during that overly long passage downtown from Seventy-fifth Street by bus? Had she alighted en route to indulge her passion for hats, for antiques, for minerals, depleting her cash reserves? Wouldn't my pessimistic advisers just die laughing if I exchanged all the notable shells in my shop for a rubber check?

All the identification she showed me bore a Philadelphia address. Her check was on a Canadian bank. I wished I was dead. Nothing in my experience as a part-time worker in the store had prepared me for this contingency. All Canadians or foreigners had either paid me in United States currency or traveler's checks, and I had learned nothing of the laws of international banking. For all I knew at the time a check from another country was just so much paper.

I expected it would take months to clear, by which time this charming spendthrift might well have overdrawn her account, even though she might be solvent right now. If I accepted the check, would I face scorn in my bank on Monday when I tried to deposit it? It had been "my" bank only since yesterday when I opened the shop account. Perhaps I was ultra-sensitive but I had thought the vice president in charge of new customers had not precisely welcomed me with open arms. I was sure he took a dim view of a new venture whimsically called Seashells Unlimited Inc., foreseeing checks in the amount of five thousand clams and weekly deposits of sand dollars. Could I confirm his misgivings by marching in with a nonnegotiable check? I would never be able to live it down.

If it had not been Saturday, I could have phoned the bank and asked for advice, or sent Lois across the street to it to find out. I could also have asked whether a check on a Canadian bank could be made out for United States dollars, and, if not, how could I possibly figure out how much she owed me in Canadian money. The fact of the matter, however, was that it was irrevocably Saturday.

My accountant's office was closed. My attorney, who was away for the weekend, might have known some of the answers. Even if she did not, consulting her would have divided between us the onus of making a hideous blunder, a two-edged blunder of either declining to make a $142 sale because I did not have sense enough to accept what was offered in payment, or letting $142 worth of inventory go in exchange for a worthless slip of paper. I would possibly be darned if I did or darned if I didn't.

I wanted that sale, for it would start off my career with such a lovely bang, but I did not want to make a jackass of myself. It was a king-sized quandary. Then I thought of the perfect solution. I remembered reading about a bank located on the fairgrounds in Flushing, the sole function of which was to smooth out such international monetary problems as arose between participating nations. It was open seven days a week.

A comedy of errors started spinning merrily. I thought Lois worked for our Fair corporation and that all she would have to do would be to phone and give them her employee identification number or some other high sign, whereupon some official would speak to me and tell me to go ahead and take her check. She, not knowing I thought she worked for them, believed I had suggested that bank because it was the only one open. She did not think calling them would do any good, but she was eager to humor me and would have obeyed any foolish command in order to get her shells.

Naturally I suppressed good manners and listened to her

end of the conversation. I could not imagine why she did not tell them she was a co-worker in a jam and, please, would they help her out of it? She said nothing of the sort, which led me to wonder whether she really did work for them. If she did not, then she had tried to deceive me, and that possibility certainly did not enhance my opinion of her credit rating.

She hung up disconsolately.

"They can't help me," she reported. "They said that if I could get out there within the hour they could sell me traveler's checks for either Canadian or United States cash. They won't let me pay for them by check because, being Saturday, they can't wire Montreal to verify my account."

So there. Even a bank wouldn't take her check. I had been right to hesitate. She gazed at the shell-laden desk, and I was afraid she was going to cry. I felt pretty teary myself. I had already suggested that she let me send her the shells next week after her check had cleared; but she demurred. She would as lief send a newborn baby by parcel post as these tender things.

I had to agree with her there. I say prayers over every parcel I post, hoping it will survive the sledge hammers, the battering rams, or whatever they use in post offices to smash things. Furthermore, I was too new at the game to have any confidence in my ability to pack shells so that they would have at least a fighting chance.

There was no place for us to go, nothing to do but stare sadly at each other across the desk.

"I just can't understand the Fair," I said crossly. "Why didn't they plan this thing better? I think it's very slipshod of them."

"They gave me a hundred dollars for expenses, but of course I can't touch that. It was for gasoline on the trip down and back and any emergency repairs to the car. That boy who was in here drove me down, and his car is on its last legs. It's for whatever we have to spend out in Flushing; food, admissions, things like that."

"Admissions?" I echoed. "Didn't they give you passes?"

"Oh, no." She seemed shocked. "They don't want them to know who I am."

I got it. She would visit the Fair incognito, the better to judge the sort of reception an ordinary tourist would get. If they knew she was Lois of the Montreal office they might red-carpet her through, allowing her to see only what they wanted her to see and preventing her from getting a true picture. No wonder she had been so noncommittal when talking to the bank.

"I brought very little money of my own," she was saying. "Only about ten dollars in bills and change. One of the things I was looking forward to was coming to this shop, but I didn't expect to buy so much. I thought maybe one or two little things I didn't already have. I never dreamed there were so many I would have to have. I've just got to have them."

"I hope you will. There must be a way. Maybe the hotel where you are staying would cash your check. Do you want to call them?"

"I'm staying with my sister," she said dolefully, then brightened. "That's it! Why didn't I think of that before? My sister has a job and an apartment right here in New York. Would you take her check?"

"Yes, indeed, if she has proper identification. I'd be glad to."

"I'll just give her a buzz and tell her to grab a cab and bail me out. Start packing the shells."

She dialed furiously, but her sister, if she had a sister, did not answer. Perhaps she had merely dreamed one up for the occasion.

I hated myself for being suspicious, but I had just about had it. The highly emotional suspense was telling on my nerves. Would Lois get her shells? Would Veronica make the sale? I wished myself back in my preownership days when such a crisis would not have involved me directly. Working for McArthur, I could always avoid possible disaster by blaming refusal of a dubious transaction on the boss. Now I had no place to hide and no one to hide behind. I *was* the boss, and this was how it would be from now on. If only such a vexatious problem had not arisen until I had more confidence in myself and had learned to say no with authority, though amiably. I had handled this badly, and let the whole thing get out of hand.

Lois was not about to give up. She said her sister was not at home just then, but that she would see her that evening. She asked if I would be an angel and let them both come to the shop tomorrow morning, Sunday, to pick up the shells and give me her sister's check for them.

She is a practicing witch, I told myself, with the powers to discern my most vulnerable point. She knows how I hate to get up any Sunday morning, but most especially the one at the end of this grueling week. She has divined that I will do anything, even gamble on her Canadian check, rather than try to beat my way down here on a Sunday when there are few buses and absolutely no cabs.

Then I remembered that the young man had mentioned their parting to go their separate ways at some street in the middle Seventies. If her sister lived in that vicinity, we were almost neighbors.

SHE SELLS SEASHELLS

The sister's apartment, I learned, was on Second Avenue at Seventy-fifth, only a few blocks away from mine.

"Great," I said. "I'll pack the shells in a box and take them home with me this evening. You and your sister can come and pick them up around noon tomorrow."

I wrote my home address and phone number on a scrap of paper and gave it to her.

She, having thought of another shoal on which the project might be wrecked, said, "My sister, Lynn, may not have enough money in the bank right now to pay for all of them, so you may have to hold some until she comes up to Montreal in a couple of weeks. Could you pack them in two boxes? I'll separate the ones that must have priority from the ones I can do without for a little while if I have to—*if* there are any I can do without."

She started dividing them into groups. Twenty minutes later there were two shells, costing a dollar each, for which she could wait. As she reached out her hand to reclassify one of these, her friend, Hans, rejoined us.

"Still here?" he asked superfluously.

"Just a few more minutes," she said, frowning in concentration.

I said, "Look, Lois, you're wasting a lot of time and energy crossing a bridge that may not even be there. If your sister has enough to pay for all of them, what you're doing now is so much wasted energy. If she hasn't enough, she can give me a check for as much as she can swing, and I'll worry about collecting the balance later."

"You mean," she said, "you'd trust me?"

This struck me as being very funny. I had spent the last

couple of hours telling her, in every whichway except the traditional one of so many words, that I did not trust her.

I said, "I mean I'd trust your sister if she vouches for you. She's here in town, and I'll want to know where she works. If I don't get paid in full I can embarrass her publicly; but I would have to send the Northwest Mounties to get you. Now run along, and I'll pack up the lot and take them home with me. It's almost closing time."

She picked up a *Thatcheria mirabilis,* the Japanese Wonder Shell, colloquially called "The Guggenheim Museum" because of the widening ramp that descends from its spire. Perhaps apocryphally, it is said that Frank Lloyd Wright drew his inspiration for that building's design from this shell. The resemblance strikes people who do not even know that Wright collected seashells and used them as models. He also used them as examples in lectures to architectual students, remarking that these so-called lower animals put the higher-ups to shame. "Note the variety of their forms," he would say. "And what do you build? Split-level ranch-style."

"I'm going to take this one with me," Lois announced. "I'll pay cash for it."

And probably sleep with it beside her pillow tonight, I thought as she counted out the change from her purse.

I don't think that she would have left even then except that Hans got behind her and pushed. I started wrapping.

It was six o'clock and time to close long before I had finished. I locked the door with the new slide bolt. At quarter to seven I tucked the last and most fragile shell into a cotton nest reserved for it, and called it a day. Fortunately, I found a cab driver who wasn't off duty.

As I got out of the elevator in my apartment building I

heard my phone ringing. I rushed to answer it as quickly as I dared, remembering that I carried all of Lois's heart's desire in my shopping bag. It was Lois.

"Hi," she said.

"Long time no see," I remarked.

"My sister can lend me the money to pay you, but it'll be a check on a Philadelphia bank. She hasn't switched her account over yet. Will that be all right?"

"Sure." After all, it's the City of Brotherly Love. Also sisterly, I presumed, and Lois certainly would not involve her sister with a bad check.

"That's great. And I wondered, in order not to break in on your Sunday, if we could pick up the shells tonight?"

"Tonight? What time tonight?" I had hoped to spend it flat on my back.

"In a little while. We're just getting organized. We're going to drive out to the Fair so that I can do some of the work I was sent down here to do. We'll stop by on the way."

"Okay. Ring the bell for apartment 5A and I'll buzz you in."

I went to the kitchen, lit the broiler for my lamb chops, and mixed myself a good stiff martini. I wished there were someone I could blame for my present state of servitude. There was nobody but myself.

Before I bought the shop my life was not in charge of anybody but me. Aside from an occasional sling or arrow of outrageous fortune, I had the final say as to how I would spend Saturday night or Sunday morning. Now I had lost control. Did I own the shop, or did it own me? I knew that this was an exceptional case, that Lois was one in a million; but it was discouraging to have her happen to me so early in my career. I felt that I would never again be able to relax in my living room, putting my feet up, or fixing a second martini if I so desired. There might never be another Lois, but every day would end with leftover unfinished business of some kind. With the stroke of a pen I had signed away my freedom, and from now on I was at everybody's beck and call.

Deeply annoyed, I had temporarily forgotten the monotony of that freedom. In a better mood I would have remembered the boredom, the depressing absence of the element of surprise.

The doorbell rang. Not the downstairs bell. The one on my door. I opened it to Lois and a slightly shorter girl who seemed in an even bleaker mood than I.

This was National Let's-Get-Mad-At-Lois Day. Hans, almost at a point of not speaking to her, she said, was sulking in the car around the corner, fuming over this additional delay. I could see that the sister, Lynn, was furious at her. Lynn had enough in her Philadelphia bank account, but she had not wanted to issue further checks against it, preferring to let it lie fallow until all outstanding ones had cleared so that she would know exactly how much she had when she opened an account in New York.

If I had any lingering suspicions that this was a fake sister manifested for the occasion, they were rapidly dispelled. There was but a faint family resemblance, but they bickered like siblings, crossly yet lovingly, like two pussycats in a basket.

Lynn was mad at Lois for being so extravagant, for squandering so much money on such "worthless" objects as seashells. Hans was mad because she had blown his entire day and was now nibbling away at his evening. As for me, my martini was lukewarm.

Lynn's wallet was jammed with identification. She worked for a well-known firm in a responsible position. Besides, our shared disapproval of her giddy sister drew us together. I would have trusted her for an even greater sum than was on the bill I presented.

Lois had unwrapped a couple of shells. Lynn said, "Don't you dare. Put them back in the box, and let's get cracking."

They stood up to leave. Lois blasted me with that devastating smile of hers and asked if I would like to go out to the Fair with them.

"I can't," I said. It is always my initial response.

"Oh, come on. There's plenty of room in the car. The rain is over, and it will be a fine evening."

I was too old and set in my ways for such shenanigans. Wasn't I?

"I haven't eaten dinner," I said.

"None of us has. We'll grab a bite at one of the foreign pavilions."

The old me could have lolled about with her feet up all evening. The new me ran to the bedroom to get comfortable shoes. I didn't want Hans to get cross at me for holding up the parade. I turned off the broiler, indefinitely postponing the lamb chops, and went off to the Fair.

On the way out Lois was able to get across to me the fact that she and Hans did not work for *this* Fair but for the future true World's Fair in Montreal which would later be known as Expo '67. This seemingly frivolous girl was a landscape architect of such stature that she had been hired to design most of the external accessories, such as lighting fixtures, drinking fountains, benches, and the like. She had come down here to take notes on what was being done right or, more importantly, being done wrong out in Flushing. In short, she was a spy. I read later that the executives of Expo had sent out a number of such scouting parties so that they might benefit by New York's mistakes.

If only she had told me this sooner I would have been sufficiently impressed to accept her Canadian check without worrying about the possibly pesky international monetary details. Then she would have left the shop in due course with her shells, and I would have been home that very minute listening to a television program which would drown out the hardening of my arteries. Instead, I was in the company of three delightful young persons and having a marvelous time. I would never have met them save for the cooperation of a cowry residing in the Red Sea who winked at one of them—that, and my foolish notion that I could run a store.

Not just any store, but a bizarre bazaar like mine that appealed to people a cut above the average. Below-average people might resent having their credit questioned and retaliate by taking their trade elsewhere. From their point of view I was the villain and Lois and company should, with justification, have hissed me. I had detained Lois, I had obliged Hans to wander about alone, and I had made Lynn addle her checkbook. And yet, these marvelous kids forgave me because they figured that anyone kooky enough to run a shell shop could not be all bad.

Whenever I am tired, vexed by paper work or the computation of taxes, or rubbed the wrong way by customers, instead of wishing I had never bought the doggoned place, I stop thrashing about and float on the memory of Flushing.

In that memory the four of us are sitting under the stars in the garden of the Lebanese pavilion, eating shishkebab hero sandwiches. For the very first time I am responding to those inevitable questions: "How did you ever get into this? How

[116]

do you get your shells? Who buys them?" Not, thank heavens, "Can you make any money at it?" for these bright young people are not the type to care.

I didn't care much either, I decided as I drifted off to sleep that night. It would be all right if I just managed to break even, because the fringe benefits were absolutely terrific.

I honestly think the fact that I had found money as well as happiness that day was immaterial, but I guess it didn't hurt. I couldn't wait until the doubting Thomases heard that it was quite within the realm of probability for a crazy shop like mine to take in over $150 on a rainy Saturday.

The gods had indeed been lavish; the omens spelled out "Full speed ahead."

Twelve

I assume that most people who have not run shops in New York City know as little about the facts of that life as I did before I ate the apple.

People who rent apartments in the City have certain well-defined rights. They are entitled to a paint job every three years. Malfunctioning plumbing must be repaired. There must be some system of garbage disposal. If a landlord lies down on these and a number of other jobs, the tenant does not have to take it lying down. He can tell his troubles to the Complaint Section of the Department of Buildings and obtain either satisfaction or a reduction in rent.

Advice to landlords who feel hemmed in by restrictions: include a store, however small, among your holdings, and work out all your frustrations on the miserable wretch who rents it from you.

The faucet drips? "Fix it yourself, or let it drip. The cold water faucet that is, because we don't furnish hot water to the likes of you. If you want hot water, get yourself a kettle and an electric plate. Don't come whining to me."

My landlord's agent is really a very nice guy and a good conversationalist on a variety of topics. He becomes monosyllabic when I say something needs fixing, and the syllable isn't yes.

Since I was paying three times as much rent as a friend who had an apartment in the building, I expected at least an equal amount of service. I hoped they'd be doing me all sorts of extra favors to keep those checks rolling in. I discovered they couldn't have cared less.

I was rudely awakened as soon as I signed the lease. I asked when I might expect the painters, adding that I thought a sort of pinky beige, like the sands of Bermuda, would be nice.

The agent, Mr. Pollock, who had been about to shake my hand on the bargain, withdrew his as if he had suddenly remembered I had leprosy.

"When did you tell your painter to come?" he asked coldly.

"*My* painter! I haven't got one. I thought we'd be using yours."

Then he told me that the lessor of a store is not obligated by any law on the books to do a single thing for the lessee. Period.

I was horrified. For the sizable increase in rent over what McArthur was paying, I thought they'd give a little themselves. No landlord with whom I had ever signed a lease for an apartment expected me to move into the last tenant's fouled nest without at least making a gesture of sweeping. I had myself been a landlady when I owned the house in Connecticut, and had knocked myself out sprucing it up for each new batch of tenants. This management did not intend to lift a finger.

"I think that's terrible," I said.

"It's the law."

"But it seems so shortsighted. What if you get someone in here who wrecks the place?"

"We evict him. The law says we can if he does deliberate damage."

"But what if he does nothing, just lets it run down hill so badly that it would cost you a fortune to get it back in shape after he moves out?"

"It wouldn't cost us a cent," he pointed out. "That's the next tenant's problem."

"But, surely, you must attend to things that are the result of flaws in the building, like those three places where the floor sags. A customer's heel went clear through one of them the other day. Even if you won't paint the walls, I should think you would at least guarantee that they and the ceiling and floor are sound."

"You can lay a new floor."

"Thank you so much. And what if the lady upstairs lets the bathtub run over and the ceiling crashes down. Will you give me your permission to build a new one?"

"You won't even have to ask me," Mr. Pollock said magnanimously.

I did ask him, however, when my prophetic vision came true the week after my expensive paint job was finished. It wasn't exactly the lady upstairs but a man on the top story whose tub ranneth over. The three intervening bathrooms were replastered and repainted at the cost of the management; mine still bears the scars and blisters.

Only my most intimate friends and customers see those, of course, but the sickest part of the store is right up front where nobody can miss it. In the front of the show window, from top to bottom adjoining the plate glass, there is an eighteen-inch wide section of wall that is allergic to plaster and has chronic acne. At the time I took over there were but a few grains of plaster dust clinging to a wire mesh through which you could see wooden lathing.

I called it to Pollock's attention and he made like he'd never noticed it. At first he acted as if it was indeed barely noticeable and I was making a big fuss over nothing. Then he tried another approach, admitting that it was appalling but must have been caused by a heavy rain, thereby transferring the blame to God.

I still thought of the unknown lady upstairs as my potential troublemaker. If she, I said, had left her window open during a hurricane, why should I suffer from the agency's policy of renting to idiots? That wasn't the way Pollock saw it. The rain had poured in through a slit in the portion of the facade that was my domain. He led me outside, squinted upward and claimed to see the point of entry. My eyesight was less keen.

"We'll probably never have a rain like that again," he said consolingly.

I doubted that we would. I mean a rain that falls straight down to within eleven feet of the ground then abruptly turns a corner and slips through a slit as though through a needle's eye happens only about once a century.

I got a different diagnosis from my boss painter who blamed

the condition on a sweaty pipe within the wall. He said the only cure would be to plaster the daylights out of the section, building a dam against the seepage. One of his minions spent three $16 hours doing just that.

The dam held pretty well for about two months, then the first trickling flake of Bermuda-sand pink paint indicated a relapse. We have not yet got back to the wire mesh and lathing, but it is only a question of time before I see it again. Hardly a trace of pink remains, and the area is a seething eruption of white plaster which never, never stops. Finding a daily mess of debris in the window, I thought I would go out of my mind. I owe my sanity to a passer-by who complimented me on the effect, saying it looked like a mass of coral. I thought it looked like psoriasis but have now convinced myself that, within its context, it resembles coral, and I am glad, glad, GLAD. This Pollyannaism, however, doesn't keep the floor of the show window clean as the wall comes tumbling down.

When it came time to sign my second lease, at a proposed increase of $90 per month, I again hurled the charge of structural flaw at Mr. Pollock. I told him that New York had endured a record-breaking drought throughout most of my period of tenancy, so how come it had been raining in my window? He allowed that the seat of the disorder might be a defective pipe, as my expert had said, but one that was situated in the building next door. He implied that no pipe under his stewardship would do anything that dirty.

While we are on, or near, the subject, I must get one other complaint off my chest. There is very little rent control left in New York City, but there is a sort of unwritten law that landlords of dwelling places may not capriciously hike rents to suit their fancy. There must be some semblance of pattern, some established percentages, or a schedule of improvements sufficient to justify the raise. Not so with the renters of stores. The powers that be would never dream of intervening.

And well they might not, for they stand to gain. There is an odious thing called "The Rent and Occupancy Tax" which clips the poor shop owner for 5 percent. Thus, a rise of $90 monthly means $4.50 more in the City's kitty. Insult is added to injury.

When I learned that I would have to do everything myself, I did not know which to do first, nor did I have the vaguest notion of whom I could hire to do the actual labor. I supposed there were freelance painters, and plumbers, etc., in Manhattan, but all those I had encountered were under exclusive contract to the management. My previous experiences with remodeling and repairs had been in small towns where there is a one-man monopoly in each field. You are not faced with a choice. You know them all by their first names. If it's carpentering you need, you call Gus. Joe is the man for electrical adjustments. Oscar plumbs, Jack is a tree surgeon, Harold digs wells, Walter unclogs septic tanks. Somehow, the realization that I would not require the services of these last three specialists comforted me.

I would have to find a painter and a floor layer and an electrician, but which should come first I could not guess. What I really wanted most in the world—and still do, I might add—was an old-fashioned handyman who would knock down McArthur's jerry-built and badly placed shelves before the painters came.

Until recently, the office of Mystery Writers of America had been located only a block away from the shop. Being a nonresident, that organization had also been a stepchild of its landlord and had been forced to shift for itself. I called the executive secretary to determine if she had ever found a neighborhood character who could fix little things. She had not, but she was able to recommend a painter whose bill had not exceeded his estimate. I telephoned him and made an appointment.

He remained within his estimate, which was so high that I had to clutch a counter for support when I heard it. But he was worth every bit of it, being a nice fatherly-type Italian who made me feel that all would eventually be well. Until he came and purred at me, I had been feeling more alone than ever in my life. I had realized that the phrase, "A one-man business," usually meant one man, his wife, and the kids. I was one woman, singular.

I had hoped that being a lone woman would touch flinty male hearts. On the contrary, it aroused sleeping misogynous symptoms in even the most gentlemanly of bosoms. The consensus seemed to be that if I thought I could buy a man's shop and do a man's work I should face my problems like a man and expect no coddling. You would honestly think that I had driven McArthur thence by brute force instead of with his heartiest cooperation.

Leonardo da Vinci, the master painter, told me his men should not lay a brush on the place until after the electricians had finished messing it up. He just happened to know a master electrician to whom he was glad to throw a little business. I think it was a case of scratching the back of a friend who had once scratched his. I don't believe that any part of that astronomical bill went to him, because an electrician's bill, by definition, is sky-high, their union having decided they are worth about three cents more per hour than the President of the United States. I do wish, however, that Leonardo had owed favors to friends nearer to me. One must pay hourly rates for time spent on the road and these birds nested deep in the heart of Brooklyn.

A master electrician is issued a license which he must guard as well as his life. He exposes himself to loss of the former unless he complies with every letter of the fire laws. He can be very stern with the client who wants to save a nickel, making her feel like a latent arsonist. McArthur had bypassed all this by doing his own wiring. There was a daisy chain of extension cords joining the two air conditioners, which were both plugged into an ordinary wall outlet. Strictly illegal, it appeared, not to mention impractical since such overloading would be bound to blow fuses.

It did no good to tell my Benjamin Franklin that McArthur had danced for years on the rim of this volcano without losing a fuse. It was decreed that heavy-duty cable, leading into the basement through a hole drilled in the floor very slowly by men on an hourly stipend, must be installed for each conditioner. Only after this project was completed did I discover that the one in the bathroom was of no use whatsoever and had been retained by McArthur merely for sentimental reasons. It was the first one he had bought.

The day after the electricians finished I blew a fuse when I plugged in the vacuum cleaner. Apparently there was something wrong with the wall outlet but I took great pains to keep that a secret from Benjamin when he came to present his bill. There was no sense in reopening that costly can of peas, and I manage very well without a lamp on that side of the store.

Ben's men had taken the better part of two days; Leonardo and his crew would blitz-paint the place in only one, tomorrow. I needed this day between to do the thing I dreaded most. All the renovation in the world would count as nothing as long as Susie continued to live under the radiator beneath the shop window. A new floor would be laid next week, including her rotted portion of it, which meant she would have to be quartered elsewhere, at least temporarily. The question was, "Where?"

I could not take her home with me since my apartment was (and still is) the domain of a despotic Siamese empress who would not stand for it. I hoped that Fred Braun, who was fond of her, could be persuaded to let her live out her life with him; but he said his sister was allergic to cats. I offered her to every cat lover I knew, even promising to pay her keep, but they all shied away from her. She was too old, too sick, too set in her ways to be either adaptable or adoptable.

The only alternative was to take her to a professional boarding kennel, but I knew what the presiding veterinarian would say the moment he saw her. He would urge me to do the sensible, though difficult thing. The inevitable thing which everyone with a grain of sense who saw Susie recommended, especially if he loved animals. I knew it was right, but I did not have the intestinal fortitude to pronounce the sentence. Yet something had to be done immediately. The electricians had so upset her that she had not touched her pork liver. The visitations of painters and floor-layers would be even more traumatic.

The Bide-A-Wee Home is only two blocks east of the shop. I had heard that their policy was not to destroy animals for

whom they could not find people, but to keep them indefinitely.

Braun was still working for me three days a week, Monday,
Wednesday, and Friday. I could not fire him from a job he
had held for twenty-five years, although he did not fit into the
image of what I wanted the shop to be. He had nearly driven
me batty on Monday, delaying the electricians by chatting
with them, and getting in their or my way when one of us had
to move fast. To my dismay this morning, Wednesday, he had
told me that important business would detain him elsewhere
on Friday but that he would be happy to join the painters and
me on Thursday.

I just could not bear it. I told him that the shop would be so
crowded with ladders and cans and workmen, not to mention
me and a possible customer or two, that we would be unable
to squeeze him in with a shoehorn. I said he should take
Thursday as a well-earned vacation with pay.

Far from pleasing him, the prospect made him more gloomy
than ever. I suppose he had been looking forward to a captive
audience of painters, rehearsing a few anecdotes about brush-
wielders of the past who had turned their hands to fine art.
However, painters cost almost as much as electricians so talk,
in this case, would not be cheap.

On top of that disappointment, Braun was slapped with the
news of Susie's imminent departure.

"You're going to have her put away," he said, reproachfully.

I denied this, hopefully with more certainty than I felt. I
explained Bide-A-Wee's policy as I understood it. I said I
would cheerfully pay for board and lodging as long as it was
necessary, and that Susie couldn't possibly be unhappier anywhere than she was right here.

I had already selected a box in which to transport her. I lay flat on my stomach in back of the nautilus case, groped through the dunes of damp litter, and found her. Only when I had put her into the box did I realize that I needed cord with which to tie it. I asked Braun to bring me some, which he did reluctantly, not wishing to be my partner in crime. Tears were streaming down his face. I asked if his sister couldn't take antihistamines or if he couldn't restrict Susie to his private quarters in their apartment, but he just shook his head and sobbed.

I was close to tears myself. In buying the shop had I stepped through a mirror and ceased to be the carefree, humane person I was, becoming hard, money-grubbing, penny-pinching, and unkind to old men and animals? That was the message Braun was sending me. I was inclined to agree with him.

He returned to the back of the shop, from which he called "Goodbye, Susie." I secured the knots, then slunk away. In one of my short stories, "Homecoming," the plot required me to kill a cat. I had coolly bumped off dozens of humans in my various works, but the murder of this imaginary feline troubled the old me for days. Yet here was the new me doing the deed for real just because I thought business in the shop would improve if it didn't smell so awful. How low had I sunk in my drive for riches?

The veterinarian who saw her said that Susie required two immediate operations, neither of which she was in any condition to survive. He said I should do the sensible, merciful thing. I did, and then had to endure the condemnation in Braun's eyes for the balance of the day. It was no good telling myself that Susie's condition was not the result of my neglect; that I came in too late to rehabilitate her. All the dogs and cats of my life had flourished and would cry with one voice that I was a good provider, if a bit of a pain in the neck at times, always fussing over wheezes and lumps and fleas and vagaries of appetite. I had got to Susie too late. That woeful afternoon I wondered if the same might not be said of the shop.

The next day was a nightmare of painters. It probably would have been smarter to close for renovations, but I had this fixed notion that to drop the torch might mean to lose the flame forever. Business, I felt, must go on as usual. Not quite as usual. Nor, thank heavens, as ever again except on the following Tuesday when the floor was laid, an even more harrowing procedure. There is a certain type of person who positively dotes on confusion and will do his very best to make it worse. I had customers that day never seen before nor since, swarming over the place, lifting the canvases with which the cases were shrouded, living dangerously directly below a man who was painting the ceiling. Miraculously there were no casualties, not even a drop of paint on anybody's clothes but mine. I got great globs of it.

When Leonardo and his boys had folded the canvas and stolen away I looked about me and rejoiced. The hideous cracked linoleum was still an eyesore but I kept my gaze above it, on the sand-pink walls which were exactly the shade I had had in mind, and on my new small desk painted to match. I may have been prejudiced, but I thought it was beautiful.

The following morning Braun looked very odd sitting behind that desk, not just because I had not expected to see him. He was officially opening the summer season on this June 23, wearing his Palm Beach suit, black tie, pearl stick-pin—but not his Panama hat. Not any hat at all. This was the only time I ever saw him without it.

His hair was thick, like marcelled stainless steel. His forehead was higher than I had imagined it. His skin looked sallower against the steel gray than it had beneath the black Homburg, and his eyes were so stricken that I thought he must be seriously ill.

"I thought you weren't coming in," I said. "Didn't you have something else to do today?"

"Later," he said. "I'll be leaving shortly."

He stood up slowly and shuffled forward to assume a familiar stance, one elbow propped on a showcase, peering out into the street, like a figurehead on a ship, trying to sight customers who rarely surfaced.

"Doesn't the place look pretty?" I asked. I thought he might at least have said something about it.

"I'll be leaving shortly," he repeated. "It's very pretty."

"Are you all right?" I asked, alarmed. He was the very picture of tragedy.

"I slept very poorly the last two nights. I kept thinking about poor Susie."

"But poor Susie was suffering, Braun," I protested. "The doctor said it was the only thing to do."

"Nevertheless," he continued as though I had not uttered a word, "I arose very early this morning so I could come down here and pack up my things."

"Pack up your things? Why should you do that?"

"To take them home with me. You don't want me around here any more than you wanted poor Susie. You told me to stay away yesterday . . ."

"That was because the painters were here. You would have been crushed to death. It was a mob scene."

He shook his head, saying, "No. You just didn't want me."

"But I need you, Braun. I don't know the names of one-tenth of the shells that are around here, and I need you to tell me which suppliers to order what from."

"You'll manage," he said tersely, and turned his back on me.

I continued to plead with him as he stuffed the accumulation of years into a Gladstone bag, but I'm afraid my heart wasn't in it. I had new crises aplenty to face each day. Need I also contend with a temperamental old man who must be handled as skillfully as a spiny sea urchin? And yet, I felt like a beast. With my fancy ways, my pink paint, and my tiny desk I had derailed this man's way of life. He loathed the new era, and I had eradicated as many traces of the old as possible. I supposed he thought I would also eventually make away with him and was simply beating me to the anticipated punch.

He put on his Panama and I wondered what had motivated his taking it off. What devious symbolism had made him choose to spend uncovered these final hours in the phase of his life he was leaving forever? I will never know.

"Let me pay you for the three days work this week," I said, reaching for the checkbook.

"Two days," he corrected me.

"No, three. I told you I'd pay you for yesterday."

"I won't accept it. Let's say that I officially quit the day before."

"If you insist."

"I do."

I gave him the check. He shook my hand and, with apparent sincerity, wished me luck. Then he was gone.

I have never felt quite so alone.

Thirteen

Although the stock was so low and what remained was mostly colorless, I had exercised great restraint in buying, timing my first large order to arrive just after the last repairman left. I made it on the nose. Ten heavy cartons were set down upon my new floor the day after it was laid. I doubt if the old one would have held them.

McArthur had left me the names of only three suppliers who seemed to be still in working order. He had dealt with each of them within the past year while other invoices, crumbling to dust, bore dates in the 1950s, even the 1940s. Several bore the names of dealers I knew to be no longer among the living.

That is one of the scary things about the shell business.

SHE SELLS SEASHELLS

Many people in it are on their last legs, and we need a trans-fusion of young blood, but fast. It is particularly perilous if an elderly shell man has been secretive about his sources—as every one of them, naturally, is—or if he has some special technique of processing shells, the secret of which he plans to take to his grave.

An ancient gentleman in Florida is the world's champion polisher of *Turbo sarmaticus,* commonly called the South African Turban. Moreover, he knows the single smooth spot in the bumpy waters off Capetown in which the shell can grow into something worth polishing. His finished work is a joy to behold, a swirl of tortoise shell and black flecked with silver. Even the most confirmed purist of a collector who publicly sneers at polished shells probably has a sample of this handiwork hidden in the back of his cabinet.

I had been out of touch with the world of shells for some while, but since he was described as a very old man at my earliest hearing I assumed he was long since gone. (I later learned he was still with us, but had an exclusive contract with a jumbo of a Florida dealer from whom I do not buy.) I had dreams of glory in which I discovered the heir to his artistry and produced enough *Turbos* to please everybody. Thus when a firearms supply house in Capetown wrote offering me shells (one does run into the most amazing tie-ins), mentioning the figure of one hundred Rands per one hundred *T. sarmaticus,* I leaped at the chance although the only Rand I knew was Sally. They also wanted to be paid by an irrevocable letter of credit, which sounded so terribly drastic and, well, irrevocable that it frightened me out of my wits. Nevertheless, I wanted those shells, so I went ahead and ordered them.

What arrived, in due time, had obviously lived in a tougher

section of the ocean than that known to the old Florida champion. These bore the scars of countless brawls with the waves. I could poke a finger through the spires of many, so I doubted they would be able to stand up to a polishing wheel. However, stubborn and hopeful to the last, I selected two sets of ten of the best and parceled them out to polishers who did what they could with them, which wasn't much but may have been as good as the champ's first effort. I'm sure a long series of trials and errors led to his finally successful process. I hope he has sealed the data in an envelope to be opened after his death, but I don't think I'll give my boys a second chance unless he also bequeaths the name of the contact who knows where the good ones live.

A Rand, I learned, was worth about seventy cents at that time. The *T. sarmaticus* operculum is one of the most attractive, with its face like a cluster of ivory pinheads, its back like a spiral of mahogany-colored leather. I was able to get fifty cents each for the percs. I even sold some of the shells. An old song guarantees that there is a girl for every boy in the world; likewise I can state that no matter how beat, how downtrodden a shell, some day someone destined to love it will walk into the shop.

Counting the initial cost, the shipping charges for that long haul, the amount I paid the polishers, I don't believe I lost too much on the deal. I may even have made a buck or two. My accountant points out that that doesn't pay the rent, but, being a philosopher, he adds that I should chalk it up to experience.

By now my chalk is worn down to the nub, but in the early days I did not make such mistakes. Not, mind you, because I was incapable of them but simply because I was too impatient to get cracking to order from afar and dealt solely with established middlemen in the United States who would send me good material, well packed, promptly.

Fortunately the three names given by McArthur met those requirements. One was a vast enterprise in Florida which calls itself "The Shell Factory," from whom I could obtain the commoner and indispensable Indo-Pacific shells, as well as Caribbean and Southern Atlantic corals and sea fans. (Fans are also corals, of a soft type, produced by tiny animals and not vegetational seaweed as some believe.) Another supplier, also in Florida, was John Root, a wholesaler whose specialty is polishing shells. I would urge him to challenge the champ in a bout with *T. sarmaticus* if I could provide him with good ones. He polishes everything else that is polishable on which he can lay his hands: from the Philippines, Green Turbans, Giant Clams, midget clams, dozens of other kinds including the Chambered Nautilus which he also neatly bisects to expose the chambers; from California and Mexico, abalone; from the rivers and lakes in the center of our country those pearly, sometimes pink beauties that are commonly called Fresh-water Mussels or Fresh-water Clams but who should answer only to their proper name of naiads, after the water nymphs of Greek and Roman mythology.

Once upon a time, before Mississippi River mud got too thick for them, that river teemed with naiads; now they can exist only in the tributaries and side shoots. Once upon a time, before the invention of the cultured pearl, a lazy river-bank character could turn a profit shelling naiads, for some might yield fresh-water pearls, then much in demand. Any one of the number of button factories in the area would buy the shells from him, for that was in the days B.P. (Before Plastic.)

Nowadays, few people know there is such a thing as a fresh-water pearl, and the button factories no longer toot their whistles. There is a happy O'Henryish ending to this apparently sad tale: Japanese cultured-pearl producers have found that their better pearls are built not upon a grain of sand but around a tiny pellet of Mississippi River naiad. Therefore they import about seven hundred thousand tons a year of the stuff, putting the old river-bank character back in business.

That is the only kind word you will ever hear from me about the cultured-pearl manufacturers, and in my book p–l–a–s–t–i–c is a seven-letter dirty word because of the havoc both have wreaked on the shell trade. Before the Japanese discovered how to cultivate oysters and encourage them to produce pearls of uniform size, pearl fishing was a lucrative profession not only in that tiny country but throughout the Indo-Pacific region, all the way to the Red Sea.

Vast fleets roamed the area in search of *Pinctada margaritifera* and *Pinctada mertensi,* the oysters capable of producing the most valuable pearls. Expert divers, who were usually the sons and grandsons of experts who had trained them from babyhood, became so *sympatico* with their prey that they were able to recognize, at a glance, the sort of habitat they would choose if they actually were oysters. Then it was "Throw out the anchor!" and men overboard until each gathering pouch was filled to capacity. Into corners where *Pinctada* would not fit were tucked cowries, volutes, cones, and anything else within reach in this happy hunting ground to serve as snacks and souvenirs.

Then it was time to shuck every pair of the *Pinctada,* praying that it contained a pearl. Most of them did not, or yielded ones disappointingly small. But this was a gambler's life wherein one lucky break could end economic worries forever. A pink pearl, a black one, or an unusually large and perfect white would fetch a fortune. The empty oyster shells could be sold to a button factory, the snacks tasted delicious, and the souvenirs could always be sold to some sailor off a ship; so who minded the constant presence of hungry sharks?

Then the cultured pearl reared its nacreous little head. Only an expert with a strong magnifying glass could distinguish the best of these from the old orientals, as naturally formed pearls were called; even those that belonged in a lower than top drawer could fool the layman. The pace of life quickened and few people were willing to add a pearl a year to little Mary's necklace so that she might wear a slim, elegant strand of them at her debut. Little Mary bought yards of them out of her allowance while still a teen-ager. The realness of "real" pearls lost its magic to all but a small band of holdouts as the cultured, simulated, and frankly fake became bigger, better, ubiquitous, and quite socially acceptable.

People consider my vocation an odd one but how about that of the woman I once met whose career was the stringing and wearing of real pearls? Annually she would visit stately homes to restring Madame's necklace, remaining as long as necessary as an honored and highly-bonded guest. Or she would visit banks and take the pearls out of the vaults for an airing. Oriental pearls, it is said, must have contact with warm flesh at frequent intervals or they lose their lustre. The estates of dowagers rich enough to own such baubles are sometimes tied up in the courts for years. My acquaintance would "sit" them, as one "sits" babies or pets, taking them somewhere nice like the opera or Symphony Hall to bring a little color back into their cheeks. I suppose the poor dear is now obsolete.

Also obsolete are the divers for what are now called

"random" pearls, as opposed to the steady reliable ones that grow in rows like corn. There is even a new process that bypasses the oyster completely, one in which layers of liquefied naiad nacre are built to the required circumference. Not to mention an absolutely gorgeous phony made out of sardine scales! Farewell, *Pinctada margaritifera!*

When the bottom dropped out of the pearl market, the pearl fleets did not instantly become extinct or extraneous. There remained a demand for pearl buttons, p-l-a-s-t-i-c not yet having been invented. These were made not only from *Pinctada* but also from *Trochus niloticus,* a pink, black and white top-shaped shell that pares down to a satiny mother-of-pearl. The common name for this is Commercial Top shell, and many a South Sea Island economy revolved around it.

Since discovery of a precious pearl no longer guaranteed a rosy future, few men could be induced to risk their lives diving among the sharks. Moreover, the ratio of man-hours to hand-gathered shells whittled down the profits. Dredges which could scoop great fistfuls of shells and debris from the ocean floor were necessarily invented.

This period, shortly after World War I, was the golden age of conchology, for the indiscriminate dredge caught as many non-nacreous shells as otherwise. These were sorted out on the homeward voyage and delivered to a merchant who had done his homework in the science, one who knew a rare thing when he saw it and was willing to pay for it. Dredging restored the element of chance to an otherwise routine business, for a valuable shell could net the captain as much as a comparable pearl; but the odds were weighted against him. "Rare," as I have said, means hard to find, and most often the haul was worth only pennies. The major source of income was the button factory. Now, when billions of people have become conditioned to buttoning up their overcoats with you-know-what (not to mention zippering their unmentionables with same), only a nut, a dilettante, or a zealot would take a boat out solely to collect specimen seashells. It simply is not a paying proposition.

Japan was once the best provider of shells to the dealers of the world. Emperor Hirohito, thoroughly grounded in marine biology, was a collector of shells and instilled respect for them in his subjects. The waters were full of *Mollusca;* there were hordes of people otherwise unemployed with time and inclination to gather and clean shells, and there were many dealers willing and able to catalogue them. Inexpensive species were exported literally by the ton. Some, I must admit, should have remained in their beds, for a high-sounding Latin name on a list may belong to an undistinguished little bivalve only its mother could love. Emperor-worship and reverence for things he reverenced was sometimes carried to extremes. Many of these little nothings remain in the old McArthur stock, but the things I want from Japan I cannot obtain.

What I want most is purple scallops. Don't tell me you've found purple scallops on the North Shore of Long Island, because unless you've seen a purple *Chlamys nobilis* from Tosa Bay, Japan, you have never seen purple. There are three other aristocrats in the *C. nobilis* tribe: red, yellow, and orange, real orangey orange that is the least uncommon. Red and yellow I have never seen, but I doubt if they could rout purple from my heart. Some of the commoners in the family are very prettily colored, a mixture of smokey mauves and roses, but those four, I know from hearsay and personal experience, sing. People will gladly pay $10 for a purple. What's more, returning travelers have told me they are paying the equivalent of that in yen today in Tokyo.

No wonder Japanese wholesalers no longer bombard us with lists; they have all become retailers. In their current affluent society wherein every man is an emperor they can readily sell every shell that comes to hand right there at home, without messing around with packing and shipping and bills of lading. Fewer come to hand, of course, and those that do cost more. The coolies who used to spend hours taking the meat out of cowries are now employed in transistor-radio factories, earning enough to buy any shell for which they have a yen. (No pun intended unless you like it that way.) The depths of Tosa Bay, which was once jammed with pearl boats, are now relatively undisturbed, except by a few amateur or extremely selective professional conchologists.

Another casualty of the plastic invasion must be mentioned. Not a week goes by but some poor soul comes into my shop and tells me he has just bought an antique table, screen, box, or what not on which some of the mother-of-pearl inlay is missing. There is very little I can do for him. I can only sell him single valves of *P. margaritifera,* which are too thick and rigid to suit his needs. Those thin, pliable fragments used in mother-of-pearl inlay were the by-product of the button industry, cut by the button-making machines to a sliver and sold as scrap. In Victorian days, when costermongers first covered their clothes with pearlies, there was an awful lot of scrap available to the artisans of Brighton, who thought of innumerable ways to utilize this waste material which was too pretty to throw away. Now the shoe is on the other foot, and a lost petal on a papier-mâché picture frame is gone with the wind.

When I was new at running the store I was terribly embarrassed when someone asked for something I did not have. I had stuck my neck out, calling the shop Seashells Unlimited. They had every right to glare at me when I admitted that I did not have a decent Venus Comb Murex to my name. It was as though I had invited them to dinner, promising Epicurean delights and then opened the door of a bare cupboard.

Now I can look them squarely in the eye and say I haven't got something without batting a lash. This is not because I have lost the slightest iota of interest and am no longer so eager to please my customers. It's just that I have learned to know when I'm licked. I used to think it was my fault when I could not produce the item requested. I thought that if I were just a little bit better qualified for the job I had undertaken I could quickly amass a worldwide list of contacts from whom I could obtain an uninterrupted flow of material. I have learned that the hazard—and charm—of my line of work is that I can never pick up the phone and order another gross of merchandise.

One must constantly battle a formidable array of foes, against whom one does not have a Chinaman's chance. Take China, for instance, since I have already said my say about Japan. I can get a few things from Hong Kong and Nationalist Chinese Formosa, but those thousands of miles of coast along the mainland which teem with choice specimens are so much dry communist land on my map.

Thus a country's ideology as well as its economy sometimes blocks the way—like Cuba's. There is a tree snail that lives only in the Oriente Province of Cuba which must be seen to be disbelieved. The colors of *Polymita picta* run the gamut from creamy white through butter yellow, mustard, pimento, grape, and maple sugar to black bean. I think of them in terms of edibles because it delights me to know that these prolific and voracious little devils are devouring the Oriente forests nibble by nibble.

Once there was population control, when millions of the snails were annually shipped to Florida where they were wholesaled by the gallon at less than a penny apiece. Then came Castro, and the flood slowed to a trickle. For one terrible month in 1965 there were none to be had, not anywhere, until someone found an unopened crate in the back of his storeroom. These vanished shortly after being placed in circulation, and all one could get were rejects, culls. I keep what good ones I have under lock and key, like the crown jewels. Soon, I fear, there won't be any, although one hears intriguing stories about their being smuggled out in diplomatic pouches and sneaked over the Mexican border into Texas. I have even heard that they have been successfully colonized in Mexico but I doubt it, although some of the culls I have received lately could be a decadent third or fourth generation who lack the fire of their forebears. I don't believe they would thrive anywhere else, but I'd bet they are flourishing in Oriente Province.

Dr. William J. Clench of the Museum of Comparative Zoology at Harvard University believes that the reason that *P. picta* is so brilliant is that there are no predators in Oriente from which they must hide. I find that a delightful concept. Would all of us be flamboyant if the presence of predators did not make us choose to be drab?

In the old days the only fauna the snails had to fear were men intent on making a buck in Miami. I'm sure everybody in Cuba has far too much to do these days to go snail-gathering, so the *Polymita* population must have got way out of hand. I would be surprised if as much as a leaf remains on a single tree.

In a small way I feel I am contributing to the liberation of Cuban snails and underdogs. There are several groups of Afro-Cubans who buy shells from me, with the obvious intention of practising voodoo with them. One large contingent, dominated by an old man who looks like a witch doctor, superimposes Christian flourishes upon a ritual that must be older than time. I can recognize one of these groups the moment it comes through the door, sometimes as it piles out of a taxicab at the curb. There are never fewer than four persons, all highly exuberant. They all chatter at once, and even though I can't understand a word they say I know exactly what shells to show them.

The witch doctor brought along an interpreter the second time he came, the first visit having proven a fiasco without one. A young woman with a good command of English pointed to a *Lambis crocata,* one of the Spider Conchs from the Indo-Pacific area, and said her leader wanted a big one of those like he used to have in Cuba.

Drunk with my own perfume, for I was learning by leaps and bounds and was darned proud of it, I told her that he was mistaken because *Lambis* was one of the few genera that did not crop up in various regions. It lived only in the Indian and Pacific Oceans and adjacent waters. There was absolutely nothing shaped anything like that in the Caribbean.

She relayed the information. The man scowled, gesticulated, and shouted at me in something that was not Spanish. The woman, who turned out to be his granddaughter, understood him perfectly and quoted him, "He says you are a stupid fool."

He took a Money Cowry out of his pocket and shoved it

under my nose while he flashed the fingers of the other hand indicating that he wanted many of them. Still being stupid and insular, I showed him a *Cypraea spurca-acicularis,* saying, "This must be the one. It's found in the Caribbean."

Her translation of his yelp was, "He says it must be yellow."

"It's called the Atlantic Yellow Cowry," I insisted, whipping out the shop copy of R. Tucker Abbott's *Seashells of the World,* a great argument settler. I turned to page 52, pointed to a picture of a tawny shell captioned Atlantic Yellow Cowry to substantiate my case. "Some of them are yellower than others," I added limply. "Maybe the ones he found were."

"He wants more yellower," she said, losing her command of English as I lost my mind. "Most yellower."

"Oh!" I exclaimed, "I think I know what you want."

What is most yellowest? *Polymita picta,* that's what. This homesick expatriate, pining for a whiff of his homeland and not knowledgeable enough to see the difference between terrestrial and marine snails, had remembered only yellow, had forgotten texture and shape.

I whipped out a box and showed it to him. All of the others beamed and giggled and nodded their heads, probably recalling happy, shady picnics in the now defoliated forest. Only the man did not join in the merriment. He said, "Baghhh," to me. It lost nothing in the translation.

I gave up. If the man insisted on placing Money Cowries in the Caribbean, how could I convince him that the nearest they had ever come to it was Africa? Not West Africa, mind you, which would have been but a short jump away, but East Africa, which meant that this tiny thing had had to hitchhike clear around the Cape. I pulled out a whole drawer full of them and let him have his way.

[144]

He smiled, exhibiting not a tooth in his mouth, and fell to it, carefully selecting twelve shells, arranging them on a counter in the form of a cross. I could swear I heard jungle drums.

And, at long last, a bell rang. I remembered a perfectly darling girl, an anthropologist, who comes to the shop once a year to buy little cowries. These will be gifts for her hostesses, the older women in the African villages she will visit on a field trip. The women played games with them, she told me, rolling a specified number of them out onto the earth, then making up stories plotted in accordance with the way the shells lay.

"Sometimes," she said, "they come remarkably close to the truth." This sounded much more like soothsaying than game playing to me, though I suppose the scientific mind does not recognize the difference.

"Like reading tea leaves?" I asked.

"Something like it, but it's a happy thing."

She told me that cowries were also used in grim things, like funeral rites, and that shells from the East Coast were in village collections up and down the West, sometimes serving as the only proof of prior communication between widely scattered tribes. Together we managed to concoct confusion for future anthropologists; wanting to bring her ladies cowries they did not already have, we decided on two species from the Gulf of California. Puzzle away, boys!

Afro-Cuban interest in shells, I now understand, is more Afro than Cuban. They may want some variety of Spider Conch, sometimes a shell that can be blown like a horn, but their major requirement is Money Cowries, and I must always be sure to have plenty on hand for them. It is fascinating to watch them make their selection from the drawer which I automatically produce at sight of them. "How did you know?" a member of a new group will ask. I just smile enigmatically and let them think that I practice a little voodoo myself in my spare time.

They will dispute each other's choices, arguing quite vehemently on occasion. There is nothing I can do to smooth these troubled waters because they know what they are doing and I have not the vaguest idea. Other customers wishing to buy a quantity of small shells will go for the brightest, the dullest, the largest, the smallest, or arrange a growth series from little to big. Not so with these *muchachos* and *muchachas* who seem bent upon acquiring as much diversity as possible. They deliberately take the bad and mediocre as well as the good.

One of my favorite group leaders, a dark majestic conjure woman with an enchanting gold-toothed smile, likes to try out her English on me. One day she mentioned her worry as to whether the cowries and cowry-built objects she sent to Cuba ever reached that lost paradise.

"I pray to Jesus they do," she said devoutly. "They *need* them there. That is where they truly need them."

I could imagine thousands of mortals needing Money Cowries as parched earth needs rain. I, too, prayed they would receive these six dozen as the woman reached between her ample breasts and took out a roll of bills to pay for them. I'm sure she's real great in the prayer department, and I will do all I can to keep those cowries rolling. Then, one of these mornings, Castro will jump out of bed and his beard will fall off. Then his ears. Then his nose. And so forth. Nothing will go right for him that whole darn day, and it gratifies me to know that a certain tiny shop in Manhattan will be partially responsible.

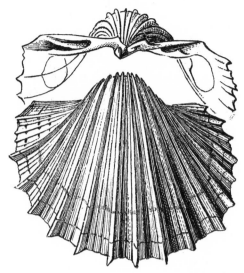

Fourteen

The third source left for me by McArthur was Purdy's Shells of San Diego, California. After a single exchange of letters I felt as though I had known Ben and Ruth Purdy all my life. Since then, although we have never met, our friendship and my dependence upon them has grown firmer.

Wholesalers exclusively, with an international clientele which includes many museums, the Purdys are not cut-and-dried business people but active shellers who get their feet wet. Their beat is West Mexico, from San Felipe in Baja California all the way down to Manzanillo in Colima, Mexico. For my taste, there are more exciting shells per fathom in that region than in any other in the world.

SHE SELLS SEASHELLS

Take *Murex,* for instance. There is not only *M. erythro-stomus* the pink-throated one, but *M. regius* whose deeper pink aperture looks like strawberry ice cream topped with rich fudge sauce. For those who just can't stand pink, there is orange-throated, brown-banded *M. brassica,* and for everybody there are spiky black-and-whites, four different species of them.

This brings up a remarkable point about the untutored shell-buying public. The four black-and-whites are called: *M. nigritus,* the commonest, from the waters farthest north, usually retailing for between $1 and $3; *M. radix,* from farthest south, a little rounder, a little heavier, costing about 50¢ more; *M. callidinus,* a fifth the size of the others with skinny spikes, like the ends of bobby pins, the prices of which begin at $3.50; *M. ambiguus,* whose spikes are like flaring ruffles, giving the entire shell the appearance of a spinning pinwheel, costing from $5 up. (I am afraid it was not called ambiguous because it looks as though it were going in both directions at once, but because for a long time its status as a separate species was moot. Some scientists considered it just a midocean melange of the northern *nigritus* and the southern *radix,* but it was finally conceded the right to a name of its own.)

It wonders me, as the Pennsylvania Dutch say, how people lured in from the street react to this quartet. At first they marvel at my ability to tell the species apart, claiming to see no positive differences among them. Yet they must see, or sense the difference because, without knowing the prices, three out of four will prefer the more expensive varieties, even though one of these is relatively small. In the topsy-turvy price structure of shells I appreciate this oasis of logic in which the prettiest costs more than the next prettiest and so forth. The only trouble is that as soon as the customer learns this lesson he may be forced to unlearn it when he sees four members of another genus whose price progression is in reverse.

If I have nothing but *Murex nigritus* to offer them, they will love it if t'other dear charmers are away. However, I wake up screaming after a nightmare in which there are suddenly no black-and-white *Murex* at all, of any kind. They are the most irresistible bait with which to hook the incipient shell-collector, male. (Females, young and old, fall for *Murex erythrostomus,* and babies take to Tiger Cowries. It is the normal thing to do. When new customers will not even nibble at the suitable bait dangled before them, I know they're not worth the trouble to catch. Too neurotic.

I think I'll stay in that parenthesis a little bit longer. One of the amusing things in the shop is to observe a young couple embarking on their lives as joint collectors. They look at *Murex*. If she likes the pink one and he the black, that's healthy, but if it's the other way around there may be trouble ahead. Both shells cost $1.50, and they have agreed to buy only one. Who will prevail? Who will concede to the other?

In only a few instances have I been able to follow through on this experiment, amassing enough data to enable me to state definitely that the pairs who leave with black *Murex* have happier marriages, but my limited sampling tends to support this theory. The contented bride, smart enough to yield grace-fully in small matters, returns in due course to buy a pink one for herself. She is radiant, and a glance informs me that I can expect her to need a Tiger Cowry pretty soon. I know two pink-grabbers who never even made it to the altar, either because she was too domineering or he was too wishy-washy, depending on which side of the story you heard.)

[149]

Conchologists divide the seas of the world into nine so-called provinces. The principal province, called the Indo-Pacific, covers the most territory. Densely populated with mollusks, it can be subdivided into four regions: the Red Sea, Australian, Philippine, and Hawaiian. While there are many shells common to all four subdivisions, some are endemic to one only. In a species that scatters its favors there will be differences, sometimes subtle, sometimes marked, between the inhabitants of two different areas.

For example, a *Conus tessulatus* from the Philippines will have rust to deep brown dots on an ivory white surface, while its cousin from Portuguese East Africa will have orange dots only. It's still the same shell, produced by the snail called *C. tessulatus* in accordance with its genes, but reacting to different environmental factors. The variation is constant, not capricious. For the shop I import this shell from both Manila and Mozambique. Should the two lots become scrambled, I can infallibly set them right again. This feat may seem flashily impressive but is actually just child's play.

I know a skin-diving Army captain who island-hopped throughout the Philippines while stationed there. Show him a *Conus magus,* he says, and he will tell you its birthplace, no matter how small that pinpoint of latitude and longitude may be. A box of *C. magus* is a motley thing, and I had assumed that each individual had carte blanche as to what color he would be and how elaborately or discreetly patterned. The captain, however, claims that each island community has predictable characteristics which you will not find in any other population.

The man in Manila who sells me *C. magus* keeps in a single bin all those he buys from roving fishermen who may have been at sea for months. There are thousands of Philippine Islands, and it would be impracticable to reserve a pigeonhole for each, assuming the fishermen were able to give him precise information in the first place.

These constant geographical variations add an extra dimension to shell collecting but learning to recognize them can be likened to earning a Ph.D. One must first go through kindergarten, then elementary school, enjoying oneself along the way, and not trying to learn everything at once, which will only lead to discouragement. This gradual sort of development is fascinating to watch. In the beginning a boy will look at a trayful of cones sweepingly and say "I have that," meaning he has something that shape, probably a *Canus spurius atlanticus* that his aunt picked up in a souvenir shop in Miami. (This is being generous to that particular souvenir shop. Most of them sell shells from the Indo-Pacific and swear by the Chamber of Commerce and all else that is holy that they are local products. Don't all shells come from Florida? That is a widely-held delusion, to judge by comments I overhear daily: "All of these shells come from Florida. All of them." Because they've seen them, or something like them in the Florida shops, and believe what they were told.)

Progressing a bit further, the youth will look at the same tray and say, "I have one like the third from the left in the second row." This is *Conus aulicus*. What he has is *Conus textile,* but they are superficially quite close. He is getting warm. When he becomes a man, he will know what he has and what that in the tray is, and will possibly be able to reel off the names of all the others.

After he has his doctorate, he will tell me whether a shell hails from Bataan or Mindanao. More likely he will berate me for not being able to give him that information. They give me a bad time, some of these erudite ones, for often the locality data I can supply is quite general except for shells I have received from amateur collectors. Commercial suppliers, in addition to storing all shells of the same species in a communal bin without regard to the points of origin, can also be coy about divulging a rich source for fear of losing it to a higher bidder.

So they glare at me, these Ph.D.'s, and I stand there with egg on my face because I refuse to invent instant data just to gratify them. I sympathize with them. They have done their homework thoroughly and they know that a cone will grow thicker in one area of its range, darker or brighter, stunted or large. What they are usually after is not tangible proof of this textbook case, but a bona fide exception that proves the rule.

I can understand that desire. I would be positively thrilled to receive an orange-dotted-only cone not from Mozambique but from Manila, accompanied by a sworn affidavit asserting its capture in local waters. I would still ha'e me dou'ts, suspecting sleight-of-hand in the warehouse, but it would give me something to discuss with the experts on an almost equal footing. In short, getting to the level on which one can recognize subtle shadings of differences gives one the most deliciously smug feeling imaginable.

Some shells make it easier for us common folk by being more or less the same throughout their province, varying individually, of course, but not presenting separable group characteristics by which their origin may be known. On the other hand some species that abide in two separate provinces can look enough alike to cause confusion. The reason is that these two particular provinces were once one. Now called the

Panamic and the Caribbean and isolated from each other by Mexico and Central America, they once formed an uninterrupted mass of water stretching from the Atlantic to the Pacific. Then Nature changed her mind and decided she simply must have a strip of land there, so we eventually had to build the Panama Canal.

Despite its name, the Pacific is not peaceful; the mollusk who wound up on the west side of the land mass had to adapt to her rougher ways. *Pleuroploca princeps,* for instance, is like *Pleuroploca gigantea,* the so-called Florida Horse Conch, seen through the wrong end of opera glasses. The Caribbean giant may be more than two feet tall, but little *P. princeps* rarely achieves one foot. A twelve-incher, however, is a giant among the mollusks of the Panamic Province, who are renowned for their beauty and intricacy rather than their heft. Exception: there is a limpet, *Patella mexicana,* which must be the world's largest, measuring fifteen inches or so in diameter. Mexicans use them as washbowls.

Panamic has no true conch to compare with the spectacular *Strombus gigas* of the Caribbean Province, but the small *Strombus gracilior* is a dead-ringer for its opposite numbers, *Strombus alatus* and *Strombus pugilis.* It would be fun to trace all these divided species back to their common ancestors. Equally engrossing is playing "find-a-cousin" for the land snails who were marooned when the earth rose up and had to substitute lungs for gills and completely alter their eating habits. The show must go on, Mother Nature always insists, and she will not take "I can't" for an answer. Just look at what happened to me when I thought I could not become the proprietor of a seashell shop: I developed gills.

Between the Indo-Pacific and the Panamic, the Japanese

Province just sits there smugly, keeping all its goodies for itself. The Aleutian Province, on the western flank of the North Pole, has very little of anything of other than scientific value to offer, and the eastern flank hasn't even a name to answer to if it wanted to raise its hand and say present.

The west coast of the United States can lord it over the east. All the way from the state of Washington to the Mexican border there is a wealth of shells in this California Province. In its eastern counterpart, the Carolinian, the upper half—*my* half—is positively destitute. It seems that our little friends were never able to get past fierce old Cape Hatteras in sufficient numbers to set up colonies, prosper, and multiply. Carolinian, from North Carolina down, is quite well to do, becoming vulgarly rich around Florida and parts of the Gulf of Mexico.

The Mediterranean Province is no great shakes, which is just as well because there are few collectors there and so far as I know no suppliers. The only divers trying to wrest a dollar from the Sea are after precious coral for the jewelry trade in Naples, and after any rival diver who so much as sets flipper on a staked-out claim. In such fin and claw competition they have no time to hunt for snails. Fortunately, the best Mediterranean shells, on the eastern rim, also crop up in the Indo-Pacific so I can get my hands on them.

The final province is the South African which is, well, South African, difficult to reach, difficult to communicate with, but terrifically beautiful, shell-wise as otherwise. It proves that we cannot blame the frigidity of northern Carolinian waters for their lackluster fauna. South African seas are every bit as cold since they are in the same proximity to the South Pole as we are to the North. (The southern beaches of

New Zealand, I was surprised to learn, are also off limits to all swimmers except those enured to chill by Antarctic breezes. I had thought one could bask on these sands the whole year round. People kept telling me that the world was round but I refused to believe them until I became interested in shells and got the total picture.)

I am aware that this division into provinces leaves out great chunks of geography, such as both coasts of South America and the west coast of Africa. The trouble is that very little is known of what can be found there. There has been scarcely any exploration and almost no documentation. Those places represent a new, uncharted frontier for conchologists, new depths to be plumbed, new shells to be classified and named.

A person who discovers a shell which he believes, after exhaustive research, to be so different from all previously named species in its genus as to justify its being recognized as a new species, may give it a name. To have any status this name and a detailed description of the shell must be accepted for publication by an established scientific journal. Then the arguments begin. If a doubting scientist argues that this is, in fact, not a new species but merely a color or form variation of an old one, the recent name is declared "moot."

The final arbiter in all such disputes is the International Commission of Zoological Nomenclature, familiarly known as the I.C.Z.N. This body and its counterpart, the International Commission of Botanical Nomenclature, are the Supreme Courts in their respective fields. The I.C.Z.N. meets formally every ten years, but briefs may be submitted for its consideration in the interim.

If the Court, in its indisputable wisdom, decides that the species is actually new, the new name goes into the books. In the majority of cases, however, the donor of the new name discovers that Linné or somebody else has stolen his thunder back in the eighteenth century. The earliest recorded name is the one retained.

The discoverer of a truly new species is called the "authority" or "author." His name follows the species name after a comma, and that is the only place it should appear. There have, however, been instances when a discoverer was so eager to affix his own name to a shell that he induced someone else to serve as author. This is considered very bad form.

There were some giddy days in October of 1966 when I thought a shell might be named for me. *Marginella veronicae,* it would have been called. (For some esoteric reason shells named for women must terminate with an "e.") I think *Marginella veronicae* has a lovely, rolling ring, but it will not be heard around the world.

The marginella episode, however, afforded me a close-up view of the economics of the shell world that I would otherwise have missed. I owe thanks to Bernard Marco for that, as well as for many beautiful shells.

Marco is a seaman, a Negro, with one of the most virulent cases of shell fever I have ever seen. He began as a customer who spent a couple of hundred dollars or so every time his ship was in port. Not indiscriminately; quite the contrary. Every time I bought an exceptionally gorgeous shell I knew that if it was still in stock when Bernard hit town he would take it away from me, and I knew it could not find a more appreciative owner.

He bought not only shells but books, every book I have on the subject which means every one currently in print. He studied assiduously on the long ocean voyages, boning up on what he might hope to find in his next anchorage.

The first shells he brought me were more promising than profitable, through no fault of his; Marco had done yeoman missionary work among the most unknowing heathens. His ship had tarried in Fortaleza, Brazil, where the natives were mad for shellfish which was present in abundance. However they had never thought of anything to do with the inedible parts except to return them to that old devil sea. Furthermore, since its destination was a watery grave, no care was taken not to damage a shell when removing the meat. The outer edge of a shell, called the lip, is its most vulnerable portion. Being the last thing built, it is like a young, green shoot. Microscopically thin in some instances, it will crumble at a touch, and these people had been attacking with fish knives.

We cannot be too better-than-thou about this. Our own efficient deep sea scallop industry follows the same procedure. Since Americans eat only the muscle, a small part of the total animal, this bit is lopped off and put into the ship's freezer while the rest is dumped overboard. This means I must import my scallop shells for baking *Coquille St. Jacques* from Ireland and Japan. This is not too much of a hardship, as the foreign varieties are actually more attractive and suitable for the purpose, but it can be embarrassing when a magazine, for instance, wants to photograph the real McCoy, and I am unable to produce it.

Although difficult to come by, I wouldn't have the heart to charge more than a quarter for a single valve of the real McCoy, *Placopecten magellanicus,* the Atlantic Deep Sea Scallop. However, what the Fortalezans were blithely discarding were *Voluta ebraea,* worth from $10 to $14, and *Strombus gallus,* costing from $10 to $25, depending upon where you do your shell shopping. *Voluta ebraea* belongs to a family called the aristocrats of shelldom. Only a few poor and prolific relations fetch less than $5, and many will leave you very little change from a century note.

More volutes come from Australia, but there are representatives of the clan in the Philippines, Ceylon, and on the west, south, and east coasts of Africa. The North American branch includes Juno's Volute, *Voluta junonia,* a porcelain white or ivory-toned beauty with square brown spots which has caused more fallings-out and blasted friendships than any other single thing in Sanibel, Florida. "I saw it first. You most certainly did not. You deliberately kicked sand over it just as I was about to stoop over to pick it up. . . ."

Southward, through the West Indies to South America, is the Musical Volute, *Voluta musica,* distinguished by its five-lined pattern suggestive of a musical staff. Then we run into the Angular Volute with its drunken cocked spire, once called *Voluta angulata,* which was easy to remember, now, thanks to the I.C.Z.N., called *Voluta dufresnei,* which is easy to forget.

To resume, in the waters off Brazil lives the Hebrew Volute, *Voluta ebraea.* Hebrew scholars claim to see every letter of their intricate alphabet etched in brown on the lox-colored background. Volute meat, I have been told, is as delicious to taste as its shell is to see, an aristocrat among lesser fish-fry, as the morel is to other mushrooms The folks in Fortaleza must set an elegant table, for I have never seen larger, richer looking *ebraea* than the ones Marco brought me from there.

The sole *Strombus gallus* rescued from the briny was a whopper too. Commonly called the Rooster, or Rooster-Tail Conch (that's the trouble with common names, which often offer multiple choices), it looks like a dancer making an arabesque with both feet off the ground.

Word traveled fast in Fortaleza that there was a loco stranger in town eager to swap cigarettes for seashells, of all things. Bernard Marco became a marked man, chased after by children and adults who usually brought worthless specimens, damaged beyond hope. Patiently he explained that the world outside was not interested in buying abused shells or mere junk from the beach. Using the best of the lot as an example, he tried to show them the difference, and urged them to treat shells more carefully in the future and to save the best ones for him.

If they learned the lesson by now they are up to their eyebrows in grade-A conchs and volutes, for Marco, due to circumstances beyond his control, has not returned. Walk, do not run, oh shell lovers, to this bonanza.

Because of some complicated thing having to do with maritime-union rules, all of it quite beyond me, Marco was forced to spend some time on the beach—figuratively, unfortunately not literally, because a true "conchoholic" like Marco will find something interesting on any beach, given enough time.

The next ship he signed on was on the West African run. He stopped in the shop before sailing to learn what I especially wanted from that area. Here arose the same old problem. I could intelligently answer the question only from the basis of my slim working knowledge of West African shells. Three names came to mind: *Cardium costatum, Marginella rosea,* and *Conus testudinarius.* These were all lovely shells, but obtainable from other sources else I would never have seen them. The best I could offer Marco was the chance to bring me these shells in choicer quality at lower prices, and that's

[159]

pretty sordid. He adores the shop and wanted to enrich it with things it would never have contained except for him. Happily, that is exactly what he did on his second trip.

His first trip was nothing to sneeze at, for he bagged several large volutes I had not seen except in photographs that did not do them justice. In one species, *Cymbium glans,* the specimens were so outstanding both in size and lustre that they almost immediately had to start traveling again. William E. Old, Jr., of The American Museum of Natural History, mentioned them in a letter to Clifton Weaver of Honolulu. He must have done a fine job of describing them because Mr. Weaver, who specializes in volutes and has written a book about them, shot back an airmail postcard by the next post saying he must have four to add to his collection. The volutes traveled from Abidjan, Ivory Coast, to Manhattan and then to Hawaii, covering about two-thirds of the earth's girth, to become part of a world-famous collection. I knew Marco would be extremely proud, as I was.

Among other things, he brought another shell I had never seen, which had the startling effect on me of making me feel tiny. This was not because it was so big, for I had seen far larger shells without feeling upstaged, but because I automatically related it to certain smaller members of its family to which my eye was accustomed. This was a *Cassis tessellata* of record size, more than twelve inches, yet seeming to be more than a times-four magnification of a three-inch Scotch bonnet. I felt as if I had wandered into one of those comic sketches wherein an adult dresses as a baby and is diminishingly surrounded by huge chairs, toys, and puppies big as St. Bernards. It took me several minutes to snap out of the fantasy, and I

could snap myself right back into the nursery every time I
looked at that shell.

Marco returned a couple of months later with three shopping bags full of shells: more volutes and a six-inch edible land
snail, *Achatina panthera,* which surprisingly lays eggs very
like those one finds in bird's nests. Most interesting to me was
a carefully packed box containing eighty-three seashells of a
species I had never seen.

There are many rare shells I have never seen nor ever will,
but I have seen pictures or have otherwise been made aware of
their existence. Common shells are a different matter, and I
thought by that time I had seen them all. Obviously a shell of
which one could get this many examples at once must be
common, so how had I missed it?

Who was asleep at what switch? This was a highly salable
item, appealing to everyone who came in while I was still
unpacking. I could have sold several of them then and there,
but I did not have the vaguest idea of what to charge, nor did
I know what I should pay Marco for them, not yet having had
a chance to discuss it with him.

I was pretty certain it was a *Marginella,* but beyond its
generic name I drew a blank. I spread them on a tray, like so
many tempting canapés, and hid them in back, to keep people
from nibbling before I was ready. Then I sat down to do a
little research.

"Research," for me, usually boils down to calling Mr. Old at
the Museum and saying, "Bill, I've got a problem." However,
as a matter of pride, I usually look through a few books first
so I can at least say, "I hold in my hand something that looks
like so-and-so. Does it ever have white dots?" This shows that
I try not to bother him all the time.

Not that he ever acts as if it were a bother. Bill Old is so dedicated to shells that the slightest hint that there might be something unusual to see sends him dashing down to the shop when his own office closes. Nevertheless, I do not want to cry wolf too often when I am confronted with a mere pussycat of an odd shade of gray. As it turned out, I could perfectly well have cried "bingo!" this time without risking an anticlimax.

Nowhere in my rather extensive library could I find mention of a *Marginella* measuring two-and-a-half inches, as these did. I called Bill, told him the size, the quantity I had, and where they came from. I added that in background color and marking they reminded me of *Cypraea cervus,* the Atlantic Deer Cowry, and that, in fact, they were so reminiscent of spotted fawns that the shell should be called *Marginella bambi.*

He said he'd be there as quickly as he could. It was like knowing the doctor is on his way after you have hurt yourself. Before I could hide the shell I'd held in my hand for reference in case Bill asked any questions, an old customer came in and spied it. A gentleman of the cloth, he has great powers of persuasion. He was determined to buy that shell, and I sensed that refusal to sell it to him would put me permanently in his bad graces. Needing all the good offices I could get, wishing to have only good reports of me sent to Heaven, I yielded.

There remained the question of price, and I still didn't have the foggiest. *Marginella* is not an expensive family, although it had recently acquired a new member in the upper brackets; *Marginella pringleyi,* from South Africa, long classified as a volute until examination of the soft parts proved it to be a *Marginella* still carries on in the volute tradition, costing dearly. I had two other *Marginella* from West Africa in the shop, *rosea* and *glabella,* priced at $3. This one was bigger, and had a aura of mystery about it, so I upped the ante and asked for $3.50. For this particular customer the price was right.

After the Reverend gentleman had departed, Marco said he'd better head back toward his ship. I wanted to pay him for what he'd brought, but again I was stumped by "How much?"

I had been shocked to learn, when I first became a retailer, that there is a 50-percent markup, that, in other words, one charges twice as much for an item as one pays for it. It sounded outrageous, and I was almost ashamed to go along with it. In practice, however, I discovered that it is essential to make that much if one is to remain afloat. With my peculiar merchandise, things are not all that clear-cut, and I must constantly fracture the rule of thumb. If I sold penny shells for two cents, or even dime shells for twenty, I'd be crushed to a pulp by the overhead. Therefore I must charge a nickel for a one-cent shell, which sounds usurious enough to land me in jail. I can't even figure out how much of a markup what that would be percentagewise. Five hundred? Two hundred and fifty? Reason totters. On the other hand, if I buy a rare shell I cannot hope to gain more than a fraction of its cost. Sometimes, if I have special ordered it for a customer, I will add only a modest brokerage fee in order to get my seed money back quickly.

Another idiosyncrasy of my line, which is not produced by good old reliable machinery, is that some things may have to be sold below cost. I buy "across the board," ordering a number of a species at so much per each, and several of them are bound to be clinkers. A shell dealer's hope is to "make out," to

[163]

clear at least as much as he invested. Believe me, adjustment of prices towards that end requires some pretty fine tuning.

I had not gone over Marco's *Marginellas* with a magnifying glass, being too dazzled by them *en masse* to get down to details; in obedience to the law of averages, some would be less desirable than others. Nevertheless, I had been maneuvered into collecting $3.50 for one within his earshot. If he knew the rule of thumb, he would expect his share to be half of that. I did eighty-three times $1.75 on a scrap of paper and came up with an appalling $145.25. Did the shop really need that much worth of a *Marginella* without which it had got along very well? But what could I do? Tell Marco to take them back where they came from? Never. I wanted him to keep bringing me shells, and that would certainly dampen his enthusiasm.

But what if Bill Old, on actually seeing the shell, said that I had described it badly and it was only little old *Marginella nothingii,* worth about a buck.

"Some of them may not be as good as the one I sold," I began, then cleared my throat and made an offer of $1.50.

Marco refused it, saying it was way too much. He had behaved that quixotic way during previous transactions. I found it so refreshing!

"Well, then, a dollar?" I asked. I was sure I could get at least that. He agreed, though reluctantly, and I made out a check. He left with it.

I did not begrudge him the handsome profit I knew he was making. Except for a few dead shells he had picked up on the beach and given me for free, he had bought all the material for small change, first from the children of Brazilian fishermen, then from the man who met all boats in Abidjan with a drawer full of samples suspended from his shoulders. As a purchasing agent he was invaluable for he was no ordinary tourist, the breed that arouses greed in natives all over the globe. I wanted to keep him happy.

Bill Old came in, and I showed him the tray of dainties. The only thing he said was, "Oh, boy!" but he kept saying it over and over as he lined up the *Marginella* according to size. I got the impression that I had something there. But what? He had never seen the shell before. He could not identify it. Few species can make those statements.

He said he would comb through all the literature the Museum possessed that mentioned *Marginella*. This might take a bit of time since the library included virtually everything, pamphlets as well as books, dealing with conchology that had been published since the seventeenth century.

I asked him what I should do meanwhile if a customer twisted my arm and insisted upon buying one. He thought $4.50 would be about right, perhaps a little more for the largest ones. He bought two for the Museum, and I added two as gifts, seeing as how I was going to pick its brains.

The New York Shell Club met the following Sunday. By coincidence, Nick Katsaras was scheduled to talk on *Marginella,* a genus he had researched in depth, of which he has a comprehensive collection, to which I planned to add a little stranger as soon as he finished speaking. I still had no name for it, although Bill had read halfway through the eighteenth century.

Nick was crazy about his present and showed it around like a kid, whereupon almost everyone wanted to own one too. Even single-tracked collectors of other families jumped the rails, and one who had strictly confined himself to West Indian shells decided that West Africa was practically next door. *Marginella* was like a new belle in town, and all had eyes for her. Word spread. I got calls throughout the week urging me to pick out two of the prettiest and set them aside. By the close of business Saturday, fewer than half of my original eighty-three remained. They were still unidentified although Bill had pushed his research forward into the twentieth century.

Marco, whose ship was still in port, was in and out all week to enjoy the excitement his discovery had caused. It was a tough fight to get him to accept another $83 from me, but I'm glad to say I won.

On Sunday the Garden State Shell Club was to meet in Newark, New Jersey. Like many New Yorkers, I also belonged to the sister organization, but had I not been a member I would have crashed this meeting. The speaker was Dr. R. Tucker Abbott, *the* Dr. Abbott of the Academy of Natural Sciences of Philadelphia, author of the Golden Nature Guide seashell book, of *American Seashells,* and coauthor of *Van Nostrand's Standard Catalog of Shells,* which is not a price list of a commercial establishment but a compilation of names and values, to be used as a standard reference work. An all-round authority, Dr. Abbott's name appears on many another flyleaf, but I was principally interested in the last-named work because the new edition thereof, then in preparation, would contain a section on *Marginella.* If my shell had a name it would be on the tip of Tucker's tongue; if he could not furnish one, it might be named for me.

I wanted Bernard to be there for the last act, which might turn out to be the curtain-raiser for a whole new show. He said he wouldn't think of missing it, so I drew him a map of the small section of Newark familiar to me, marking the Museum, our meeting place, with an X.

He got there before I did. So did Dr. Abbott, who was surrounded by a circle of admirers. I wedged my way in, interrupted him in mid-sentence, and placed a plastic box in his hand.

"Donation for the Academy," I said. "Can you tell me what it is?"

He did not hesitate one second. "Why, yes. It's *Marginella desjardini*. Marche-Marchad described it in a paper published in Paris in 1957. That had been its only appearance in print, but it will be in the revised Catalog."

Drat Marche-Marchad! Thanks to him I had missed immortality, and by less than a decade! If Bill Old had worked backward instead of forward in time I would have known right off the bat that my dream was not to come true. As it was, I'd had ten days of burgeoning hope.

Dr. Abbott was saying that the Academy would write me a letter of thanks. I was making a genuine contribution to science since they had been unable to obtain a specimen for the collection elsewhere. Such donations to museums are tax-deductible; a letter would serve as a receipt.

"Don't bother," I said, still sulking. "The amount is negligible."

"Negligible? I don't call ninety dollars negligible."

That brought me back from West Africa where I was getting even with Monsieur Marche-Marchad. In a flash I was right back there in the Newark Museum, echoing "Ninety dollars! For each?"

"For both. It's valued at forty-five in the new Catalog."

If I had been somebody else, not me, I probably would not

have rushed over to where Marco was sitting to share the joke with him. He thought it as funny as I did, and laughed and laughed. The somebody else I might have been would have buttoned her lip, telling him only that the shell had already been named, leaving out the price bit.

Marco had been dreaming that dream of glory right along with me. When it began to look as though no one had beaten us to it, we had discussed possible names. I first said I thought it should be called *Marginella marco* after the man in the field. He had modestly declined, saying the honor should go to me because if it had not been for my shop he would never have bought them from the fisherman. He would be most disappointed to hear that this Alphonse-and-Gaston bit had been totally irrelevant. I didn't have the heart to tell him the sad part and leave out the funny punch line.

A smart business type would have proceeded differently. Having cornered the market in *Marginella desjardini,* all I had to do was sit on them and wait for them to hatch. When the tip-sheet came out and there was a demand to buy, I could supply and make a mint on an original investment of $1 per shell. On the other hand, a smart business type might have felt like jumping off the George Washington Bridge. Impetuously I had parted with forty-four of the little nuggets for a mere $4.50 apiece, representing a loss of 1,782 lovely, if hypothetical, dollars. Looked at that way, I was a failure, a ruined merchant. Perhaps it was hysteria that made it seem so funny.

The point not to be denied, however, is that I could have sold, at most, only four at the higher figure. Being the kind of sap I am, I would have felt constrained to split the take with Marco and to offer him at least $20 each for the others. In fact I think that if I had been aware that the shell was "worth" $45 when he walked into my shop with eighty-three of them, I would have screamed at him to take them away. I doubted if there were more than twenty people alive who would pay that much for it.

Besides, any species of which a fisherman could obtain that many at a time cannot be considered rare. It might have been a lucky fluke, of course, the lot having been found in the stomach of one greedy fluke or a Mussel Cracker. Or these might be the accumulation of years during which the man had not been able to unload them on anyone until Marco came along. I doubted this, however, as the specimens all looked equally fresh, as though they had been washed up on a single wave after a storm or found in a colony visible only during extreme minus tides.

I asked Marco whether his contact had acted as though the find was extraordinary or routine. He said that no special fuss had been made about it. He had become quite friendly with the man, who spoke only French. When he got back to Abidjan on the upcoming voyage, he would get someone bilingual to help him. If it developed that baked *M. desjardini* was a staple in local diets, there would have to be some downward revision in the price.

I could not resist breaking my self-imposed rule. Thinking that what the man asked for the shell would give a clue as to its availability, I asked Marco how much he had paid. He started laughing again, then shared the cream of the jest with me.

Eighty-three *M. desjardini,* "worth" $45 each, had been purchased for one paperback copy of Dr. R. Tucker Abbott's book, *Seashells of the World,* which retails for $1. Try that on your abacus.

[169]

I decided to play it cool from there on in, to hedge a little. If Marco returned from his next trip loaded with *Marginella* and reasonably assured that the supply was unending, I would hold to the established price—mine, not the Catalog's. Meanwhile I would not offer them to the general public but restrict their sale to old customers and shell-club members who would be charged twice as much as those who got in on the ground floor.

The two categories that could still buy the shell constituted a large portion of the small conchological world. As I had suspected, there was much resistance among them to parting with $9 for a *Marginella*. If *they* did not queue up, how could I expect people outside the circle to pay more? I was left with a respectable number in stock when the flurry died down.

I heard that Dr. Abbott had lowered the listed price from $45 to $25, the higher figure having been based on the amount asked by Marche-Marchad back in the 1950s for the single specimen sold. I would still make a substantial profit. I could relax until I got a copy of the new Catalog hot off the press. After that, I would be able to point with pride to the recorded value and give strangers the pleasure of a bargain at less than half the price.

Publication day came and passed without causing a ripple. The trouble was that all interested parties, by that time, either owned the shell or had owned it, for some brief period in recent history, before they traded it for something they wanted more.

Talk about wampum! Some collectors will buy shells only with other shells, feeling that the introduction of cold cash demeans the transaction. Somewhere along the line they may have to use specie to obtain a specimen from a scrubby character like me, but they erase the memory and alchemize the boughten shell into ethereal gold which they can use for an exchange.

My $4.50, or $9, shells were traded all over, presumably for $45 numbers. Several of them wound up in the hands of a West Coast dealer in rare shells. I would dearly love to know what species, with a final "s," he paid for them.

This, of course, is the basis on which some of the more fantastic prices rest. I have heard someone say, "I don't know how much a *Lambis violacea* is worth in money," spitting out the nasty word, "but I know I traded a *Voluta bednalli* and a *Harpa costata* for one, and that's easily a couple of hundred dollars." On they go, taking in each other's washing while the price spiral coils upward.

It reminds me of George Gobel's routine in which he boasts of owning a $10,000 dog. "Of course I didn't exactly pay ten thousand for him," he adds, inimitably. "I gave the kid a buck and a nine-thousand-nine-hundred-and-ninety-nine dollar cat."

Maybe I could have realized a little more on *M. desjardini* if I had played my cards differently. Maybe I should have traded them for more salable cones and cowries, but I was afraid to step on that merry-go-round, the riding of which is a career in itself. Besides, can you imagine what my already sorely pressed accountant would have said? He prefers to have me deal in coin of the realm because it makes for a neater tax return.

And how would I have estimated how much to pay Marco, who, incidentally, never made it back to Abidjàn? Butterfingers that he is, he lost that ship too, and the next shells he brought me originated in Guam.

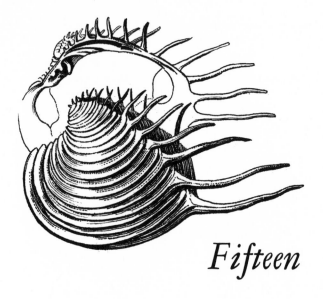

Fifteen

Although I am convinced that confirmed "conchoholics" set too high a value on certain shells, experience has taught me that the general public tends to err in the opposite direction. It is largely the fault of the conspiracy against them that seashells are regarded as Mother Nature's stepchildren. People know that gems, even semiprecious stones in unpolished condition, are worth quite a bit and will pay the bill without argument. They'll pay through the nose for mounted butterflies or beetles, if such are their fancy, but will turn white on hearing that a shell costs $3.

How low, I wonder, was their uneducated guess? The most extreme cases of this sort probably don't even bother to guess.

They've got big round zeroes on the price tags in their minds, and if I said, "Fifty cents," they would whistle and shake their heads in disbelief. On days when I get a run of this sort of visitor, although I may have started out in the morning determined to forgive them because they knew not what they did, I wind up feeling that ignorance is no excuse for being stupid. I should think their common sense would tell them that these things must have some value or they would not be for sale, would not even be here on these shelves so far from the sea.

I'm not talking about those benighted souls who think that only man-made articles are worth anything. They are beyond hope, and it is just a waste of breath to try to make real to them the man who wrested it from the sea, perhaps risking his life to do so; the one who spent many patient man-hours cleaning it properly; the one whose muscles were in his brain, which had been trained to recognize and classify the shell so that he might inform me of its existence; the minions who packed it superbly so that it reached me without a man-made mar; lastly, me, who thought it important enough to justify all this fuss. We form a team which, although we did not make the shell, at least made it available.

I am now frowning sternly at those people who sufficiently appreciate Nature's handiwork to know that an orchid costs more than a dandelion, but who nevertheless think that no shell should cost more than they are prepared to pay. Having no faith in the price structure of the shell business, they consistently try to alter it to suit their personal needs.

They have only $2 to spend, but they have this terribly large space on a bookshelf to fill so couldn't I give them that $20 Triton's Trumpet for less? It is precisely what they need, and I am an old meanie not to let them have it for a price within their budget's scope.

This is not ordinary bargaining, a practice that I so detest that I cannot indulge in it even in foreign markets where it is expected. I know some people consider it half the fun, and it may well be a sport engaged in by antique dealers and similar adventurers. However, as I have said before, I have a literal mind, and when someone says the price is $10, so be it. I am a born and bred nonhaggler, and it grieves me when I am asked to play the game. It is especially irksome since my would-be opponents appear to believe that I improvise the prices as I go along and can as easily modulate them. The chief difference between this and other forms of bartering, though, is the prevalent belief that the merchandise is really theirs by divine right; my rights, in regard to pricing, are nonexistent and/or an infringement of theirs. As far as they are concerned, none of those middlemen between me and the deep blue sea exist outside my money-hungry mind.

Believe me, the middlemen exist, and the number of links in the chain that leads from the deep to me determines the price. If I must buy from a wholesaler, a Mr. A, in this country shells he bought from Mr. B, abroad, obviously the price will be higher than if I dealt directly with Mr. B. The good Mr. B's in this business, however, are few and far between or under exclusive contract to some Mr. A who has learned how to communicate with and extract the best material from them. The bad or merely inexperienced Mr. B's require more time than I have to spare for the establishment of a mutually beneficial relationship.

They will ship immature, beachworn, even dirty shells, some with part of the animal still in them—ugh!—because, to quote my man in Formosa, "We have had shell business on this island only two year so we do not know what is shell?" I like that boy, and will be patient with him because I feel that he is trying, and he is steadily improving. Some of them are hopeless, and it's better to let a wholesaler, who has outlets for material not up to my standards, run the risks and take on the cleaning jobs. So I pay a little more? So I make a little less.

One would think the ideal arrangement would be a direct line to the diver, but herein lies a paradox. The diver knowledgeable enough to recognize what he has to offer usually has an inflated idea of its value. Most likely he is a shell nut, in a class with those rarefied buyers of rarities, which is why he bought his scuba gear and moved to New Guinea in the first place. He is completely out of touch with the shell-buying public, and if he is passionately devoted to a certain species he thinks the public will also be, whatever the cost.

I've had amateur divers who wanted to charge me twice the going retail price for a shell. (What's worse, one nonprofessional did not mail me such an invoice until after I'd sold everything at what I considered a sensible price. Ouch!) Or they will attempt their own form of block-booking, expecting me to take hundreds of something of which they have a surplus. It's no use telling them that its appeal is limited, that it will clutter up my cabinets instead of theirs, the only difference being that I would have to pay for the inconvenience. The truly devout shell nut's credo states that every shell is beautiful or, at least, interesting, and that if I did my job as well as they did theirs I would have no problem. I just wish they could bruise their shoulders against the wall of sales resistance that surrounds me daily.

There are two bright spots in this dark picture for me: my

man in West Panama, and my boy in the British Solomons. The former, a United States citizen working in the Zone, came into my life by way of a mimeographed letter he sent to a number of dealers. I, who customarily let correspondence lie on my desk until it molds, was fortunately the first to reply. My alacrity was due to the fact that he was offering *Oliva porphyria,* a favorite of mine and a sure-fire seller, at a perfectly darling price.

Subsequent correspondence revealed that Bob Shaver had suffered a pinched nerve a couple of years back and had been forced to give up golf. To fill his leisure hours he took up shelling; after the nerve healed, he had no time for golf.

Bob's attitude should be the one of all amateurs. He enjoys shelling, and, being adept at it, gets more than he is able to keep or give away. Any sums he can realize on his surplus are just so much velvet. He has read all the books, but remains open-minded about what price the traffic will bear. I do not take advantage of him. For the commoner species I pay him exactly what I would pay a regular wholesaler since these are bread and butter I would have to buy anyway. For the rare ones I listen to what he has to say about just how hard they are to find in his area. In some instances things scarce in his area will be plentiful, and therefore cheap, in other places so I will advise him to stop taking and cleaning them unless he is willing to settle for the lower amount. He usually is, because what else is a sheller going to do but shell?

Once he threw me a curve, offering me *Conus orion* (then called *Conus drangae*) which I had never seen on a price list. He said he found fewer of them than *Conus dalli* or *Conus vittatus,* giving me a criterion since I knew these retailed at between $7 and $10. Whatever daydreamers may think, life is not all skittles and beer on tropical beaches. In West Panama there are but twelve really good shelling days a year, occurring during the extreme minus tides of the spring and the fall equinox. The rest of the time the mollusks are concealed by murky water deep enough to be inviting to sharks. Within those spans, Bob could hope to find no more than five *C. orion* annually. In view of this he thought it was worth a bit more than the figure given in Van Nostrand's Catalog, which was $10. I upped it to $12, offered him $6, and he was satisfied. So was the cone collector to whom I sold it.

A few months later a wholesaler, who is meticulous about pricing within the rules, offered it to me for $17.50. Two additional links of chain had intervened. They had bought it from someone who had probably given a diver less than I paid Bob. If I had not dealt with Bob, I would innocently have assumed that the shell could fetch $35 retail. Perhaps it could, but the total of three I then had found it rough going at $12, the supply of bigtime spenders not having kept up with the demands of suppliers.

The boy in the British Solomons was a prize in a rather soggy box of Crackerjacks. First there was a lady from Brooklyn whose sister was a Seventh-Day-Adventist missionary in the islands. Their mother had recently entered a nursing home. The distant sister wished to help with the bills, but was hampered by laws against the sending of money. A happy solution seemed to be to buy shells from the natives and ship them to the Brooklynite who, in turn, would sell them to me. Lovely, lovely, except that what she sent was junk, not worth the postage thereon, for which I paid more than I should because the story was so touching. I said that I could not be so sentimental the second time around, that future parcels must contain things I could not obtain more cheaply elsewhere. The stateside sister bought a copy of Abbott's *Seashells of the World,* and I circled those species that would make this a going proposition for both of us. Two more packages of junk arrived before the lady gave up.

By then, she had started something. The students in the S.D.A. mission school where she taught had learned an extracurricular lesson and knew that shells were salable. Somehow they found my address. I was bombarded with parcels, nineteen in all, crammed to bursting. The senders apparently believed that the safest packing material for shells was other shells, which works fine for some species but is sudden death for others. All of the cones were shattered, except for the infants that had been murdered in their beds too soon, which so distressed me that I could not bear to have them around. I immediately gave them to the American Museum for study so that they would not have given up their lives entirely in vain, or for my gain. I could not possibly have sold them.

I composed a form letter, including a lecture on conservation, and typed as many copies of it as I could at a clip on my portable five times. Deciding what amount to put on the enclosed check required a delicate balance. I knew nothing about the rate of exchange in the Solomons. What I thought was paltry might turn out to be princely there, and I would drown in a sea of parcels. Obversely, I wanted to reimburse them for postage with a little to spare for a treat.

I must have shaved it pretty thin for only one of the boys wrote to thank me and his motive was slightly ulterior. This was K. Orepala, who said he had a Golden Cowry and a Glory-of-the-Sea he would like to sell me. Not one, but two big casinos. I doubted it.

When I have such doubts, and I always do, I don't monkey around. I don't want to be the one to tell someone that what he thought was worth hundreds is amply covered by the herewith check for $1, creating the ineradicable impression that I am cheating him. I bypass the shop completely and, by agreement, tell him to send the material to the American Museum, where identification has the ring of authority. I so wrote to K. Orepala at the mission, then phoned Bill Old to tell him to expect the usual battered Textile Cone and a semi-fossilized Tiger Cowry.

Early one morning, two weeks later, Bill called to say he had received a parcel containing one indisputable Golden Cowry and two, not one, Glories-of-the-Sea. I was welcome to the former, but the Department would like to buy the two cones. And, believe it or not, they bought a third one that arrived from K. Orepala the following week. You could have knocked me over with an Angel Wing. (The highly descriptive common name of fragile Florida bivalve, the Latin name of which is *Cyrtopleura costata*.)

And that's not all. The fourth *gloria,* the one that graced the shop, arrived unbidden a month later, preceded by a note announcing its acquisition which included the information that "it hasn't rotten yet. I will send it to you when it stops smelling." Then there was a fifth one, of record size but little value because it was so beachworn from years of lying on the sand unnoticed until Orepala's success made other boys more careful about what they used to skip the waves. I paid $10 for it and donated it to the Museum.

The rest was silence from K., perhaps because he was now

too rich by island standards to bother. There may be another explanation. Bill Old wrote a paper about the recent rush of *glorias* which was printed in the Hawaiian Malacological Society's magazine, the monthly Bible of shell collectors, one of whom may have kidnapped my boy. An individual could give him so much more than a dealer, like me, who must bear in mind the price limitations of other individuals. That's the chance one takes when one gets something flamboyant and newsworthy. Not that I care. I really prefer a steady flow of modestly priced shells in and out of the shop to an occasional geyser. It's more restful.

Some of my needs are met by the enchantingly named Angelica Villaluz, whose de-Latinized common name would be Angel of the City of Light but who anticlimactically lives in Project B, Quezon City, Philippines. Her grandfather was a wholesaler of shells, and she has had a feeling for them since childhood. Currently attending college, she maintains the family tradition by sending me a small assortment each month, some self-collected, some bought from fishermen who used to supply Grandpa. She never lists or prices what she sends so I must make out my own invoice. What's more, I must count the amount of postage on the parcels and convert pesos into dollars so that I may reimburse her.

The German gentleman in Mozambique doesn't invoice, either, but after two years of nagging him via airmail I won a concession. He now gives me his estimate of what he hopes to receive for the entire shipment, adding that I can give him more or less if I choose. In view of past difficulties I always choose to give him exactly the amount of his estimate.

About halfway through his folder of correspondence in my files is a harsh little note. All the other letters are enchanting

SHE SELLS SEASHELLS

for Kurt Grosch has a fine literary style with a unique flavor which is a blend of his native tongue translated into English, modified in some indefinable way by the cadence of Portuguese and whatever native dialects he may speak during the day. Furthermore, having been isolated in East Africa for so long, living almost hermitically, his diction remains delightfully archaic. His subject matter is pretty fascinating, too, for he can refer nonchalantly to tidal waves that flooded his living room and soaked all the labels off his shells, and he frequently returns from the post office to find a lion in his garden.

He writes on a typewriter, not with a quill although it reads that way, by the light of an oil lamp, usually after a trip to the post office where he either received a check from me or mailed me a parcel. If the latter, he does not tell me what to expect, merely that four-hundred-and-some-odd shells are on the way, leaving me about eight weeks in which to guess and wonder whether I should order certain items elsewhere. Fortunately he puts a list inside the package so that I will know what I have when I receive it. Some of the species he sends are pretty obscure and would take hours to identify. He also tells me how many of each to look for, and I do mean "look for"; Mr. Grosch's earliest shipments were like treasure hunts.

Packing material is at a premium in Mozambique. Boxes are harder to find than rare shells, several of which may accumulate before a proper container is found. The usual accoutrements, such as excelsior, cotton, or tissue, seldom come to hand. During the dry season one can obtain sawdust from the lumber mill, but it rains most of the time and soggy sawdust adds to the postage.

Mr. Grosch's favorite was rice husks, until the United States postal authorities turned thumbs down, I presume at the behest of the Bureau of Agriculture or some such busybody. Incidentally, there are no laws against the import and export of seashells. In fact most countries make the transfer of such scientific educational material easier by including a paragraph in their customs codes exempting them from duty charges. It's the vegetation that gets the cold shoulder because it might be a carrier of pests or plant diseases capable of infecting local produce.

I felt some personal concern about pest control when I learned that husks were heading my way. They would, I expected, be filthy and full of crawlers who would take over the shop. I armed myself with an extra can of bug spray, quite unnecessarily it turned out, for they proved to be clean as a whistle. Every last bit of edible rice had been threshed out of them; a stowaway insect would have starved to death on the voyage.

One of the bad things about husks, however, is that they themselves resemble dead bugs. Whenever I hear a startled little cry, I know that a customer has picked up a Mozambique shell. Husks seep into the cavities like water during the long journey, and no matter how violently I twirl the specimens on arrival, some scrap inevitably remains to leak out and startle the unwary.

Unpacking an early Grosch box was a tedious adventure. I would dig in, take a handful of husks and let them trickle between my fingers, only now and then being rewarded by a shell for my pains. Yet shells were sprinkled through, like raisins in a fruit cake, and each had to be checked against the list lest one be thrown out. The first time, being leery of the husks, I quickly removed from the premises all containers of those inspected as soon as they were filled, then had to retrieve them from the garbage can for a second scrutiny because the count was short. Some of the specimens were minute; it was one of the smallest that became a bone of contention between me and Mr. Grosch.

Cypraea punctata, at its mightiest, measures one-third of an inch. Most people have to put on their specs to see this pale beige shell and the tiny brown dots that cover it and give it its name. In a shipment that included thirty of them there were thirty-two other assorted shells but no hint from the sender as to what he hoped to get for the lot. Since he had never assigned a price to a species and had only told me—when he remembered to mention it at all—that such-and-such number of shells should bring x number of dollars, I had assumed that this was how things were done in East Africa. I had thought he bought from divers at so much the piece, without regard to individual value. To find a guide I scanned his letters and found one in which he mentioned an optimum price for one hundred and twenty-five shells. I divided the sum in half, and mailed him a check. Then came the letter different in tone from all the others.

A diver, he chided, had the right to expect a bonus when he found rare shells since so much of his take was drearily routine, and so much of his time was lavished on the finding and cleaning of shells worth only pennies. The only incentive that keeps him going is the elusive, though not impossible, lucky strike that will net him some folding money. If divers were to be paid no more for specials than for common ordinaries, they would be fools not to quit for some pursuit with greater stability.

Mr. Grosch put far more schmaltzy hearts and flowers into his letter than I have dared to extract. When I had finished reading it I felt like a White Imperialist growing richly fat on the sweat of my African brothers. (Question: Does one sweat under water?) It appeared that my recent check had covered only half the value of the *C. punctata* alone.

I upped the ante and the price at which I had planned to sell the cowries. Thanks to Grosch, I now knew what it was worth. The diver must have known from the beginning. The general public, alone, thinks $2 is exhorbitant and that 50 cents would be more like it. In two years I sold seven to people who knew the shell and its value. I needed twenty-three more such experts.

I took a loss on that deal, but it was minor compared to the *Tibia* catastrophe. *Tibia* is a small family, three members of which reside in the Philippines. One of these is *Tibia fusus,* the Shinbone Tibia, a highly improbable shell suggesting a unicorn's horn. If the designer of this had shown me a preliminary sketch I would have warned him it would not work, that the aperture was far too small and the long, skinny tailpiece was quite impractical. The first one I saw, about twelve years ago, cost $40 and seemed a bargain. An equally perfect specimen today would run to about $15. Its distinctiveness led to its downfall. Any casual frolicker in the waves, who had seen one and been told there was a ready market for it, could recognize the next one he saw and grab it. Everybody and his little brother became a supplier of *T. fusus.* The price plummeted.

The *coup de grâce* was delivered by the merchants who came to the Flushing World's Fair bearing bundles of them which, toward closing time, they unloaded at panic prices. Unlike cones or cowries, which are so varied that one may go on buying them forever, like peanuts, a *T. fusus* is a *T. fusus;* one buys the best one that one can afford, and that's the end of it. Consequently anyone shell-minded who visited the Philippine pavilion left with his lifetime supply.

Then there is the small *Tibia powisi,* nice but not sensational, and the more recently rediscovered, therefore highly priced, *Tibia martinii,* which lives two hundred and seventy-five fathoms down off the island of Marinduque. In all of the Philippine Islands there was but one dredge capable of functioning at that depth. I think its owner must have worked it day and night during the intervening years, thereby killing the goose that might intermittently have laid golden eggs. If only he had known that more eggs mean less gold.

T. martinii was selling, if at all, for $150 in the summer of 1964, when a nice young Filipino walked into the shop and offered me six of them. He also had twenty-two *T. fusus* and two dozen *T. powisi.* That would be $900, he said, and I could pay him by check.

That was it. There wasn't a doubt in his mind but that I would clap my hands for joy, jump up and down, possibly embrace him. He was dumfounded when I told him that I didn't want any part of his treasure, except perhaps one *martinii* to lend the shop tone. I would pay $75 for that.

I was still so insecure as a dealer that I quivered when he tut-tutted me. He picked up a copy of the Van Nostrand Catalog, opened it to the *Tibia* page where *T. martinii* was listed at $90. So, also, was *T. fusus,* due to a typographical error. I tried to explain that this was like citing a stock-market quotation from a year-old newspaper, but our minds could not meet.

He was a nice boy. After the anger aroused by his acute disappointment simmered down it was a pleasure to have him around. Soon he was telling me his troubles, and they were sizable. He had come to this country to go to college; back in

Manila he had invested a large chunk of his tuition money in *Tibia,* expecting to triple it. Now he did not know what he would do.

I felt sorry for him and furious at his countryman who had sold him the Brooklyn Bridge. I advised him to cable the fellow who fleeced him demanding his money back, then to wrap the shells carefully and return them. Such villainy must not be allowed to triumph.

The fellow was not a villain but a friend, my friend said reprovingly. He had sincerely believed that the shells he sold would fetch three times as much from our affluent society. Had he not seen that fabulous figure in print?

In this case a little knowledge was a disastrous thing. He knew how much a *T. martinii* was theoretically worth, but he did not know how limited its market was. *Martinii* is not the beauty that *T. fusus* is, except in the eye of the sophisticated beholder, of which I suspect there are no more than a hundred extant. Furthermore, of this number, ninety-eight probably already possess the shell.

You men might just as well stop dredging off Marinduque Island, for I was able to fill those empty slots in the cabinets of numbers ninety-nine and one hundred. Being soft in the heart and head, I finally broke down after two weeks of entreaty and bought the whole lot, giving the boy no more than he was out of pocket and an admonishment to let this be a lesson to him. On the surface it would appear that I got a bargain, but three years later I still had sold only two *T. martinii* and none of the others, of which I already had more than enough.

Sometimes it seems as though the rare-shell collector is a member of the rarest species on earth. It is a truism among conchologists that no shell is really rare, that unknown areas must abound with it or it would by now be extinct. The case of the collector is somewhat different. He suffers from under-nourishment. He does not know that his desire for things from the sea is a normal and healthy one with several centuries of tradition behind it. He considers it a vice peculiar to himself, and keeps it secret. He cherishes his cache of whelks and oyster shells, and thinks that is all there is and that no one else cares.

Feed this poor unfortunate! Get your nearest museum to exhibit the stuff it has stashed away in drawers. If it hasn't any shells, make it feel ashamed of itself. Or you could open a shell shop, or see that someone in your community does so, or at least takes a step in that direction. I don't think it would be possible to start a shell store from scratch, but a beginning can be made in a corner of some already solvent establishment. Study a bit first, so you will know what you are doing, then specialize in a single species or several species from a single area. You will absorb knowledge through your pores and soon be able to cope with a larger inventory.

However, please let it consist of pure shells, not things made with them or shells made into things. Don't be a party to the notion that shells must DO something or be done unto rather than merely being allowed to be.

It may seem odd that I should encourage competition. The truth of the matter is that I'm tired of the obligation of being old Mother Seashell to practically the whole world. It gets pretty silly when a lady in Hawaii writes to a shop on Third Avenue in New York City for a South Pacific clam she has seen pictured in a magazine. She ought to be able to find my counterpart in her yellow pages.

The children's letters break my heart. Writing in pencil on

ruled paper, they ask for a list of the shells that I sell. I don't
do mail order so I send them a mimeographed letter listing
several dealers who do, knowing this will not help them
because what they will receive is an alphabetical listing of
Latin names that will be so much Greek to them. I once tried
to coax a mail-order dealer into issuing a special list for kids.
He admitted that it was a nice idea but that it should be
undertaken by some nonprofit charitable organization since it
would always be deeply in the red.

He was right, of course. Even the most generous of allow-
ances will not permit children to buy shells sufficiently costly
to keep a dealer in business or—more importantly—to keep the
divers diving and the dredges dredging. The older folks simply
have to wake up and see what is in danger of being lost before
it's too late.

When I launch forth on this subject, someone is bound to
ask if I am not afraid that a sudden demand for shells might
depopulate the oceans of molluscan life. I reply that the ocean
is deep and wide, and that there are more shellfish in it than
ever came out. Strict rules of conservation must, naturally, be
observed, but if a tenth of the gorgeous specimens that are
thrown away or abused were made available there would be
enough for everyone.

And what a shot in the arm it would be for the emaciated
economies of depressed areas! Government officials in some of
the newer African nations, suspecting that commerce in seashells might contribute, however infinitesimally, to the
national income, write to inquire what kind of shells I want
and how much I will pay for them. I can only ask them to
send samples from which I can evaluate their judgment of
shells as to quality, condition, and variety.

SHE SELLS SEASHELLS

I always stipulate that the parcel be small, remembering with horror a running newspaper account of an Englishman who wanted a few shells for his Battersea mantelpiece. Through its embassy in London he contacted the Trade Commission of a burgeoning republic, requesting a few shells. He received a ton-and-a-half of beachcombings, priced unrealistically high, on which the charges for shipment and truckage from the dock were staggering.

There is a lovely shell shop in London called Eaton's, but the man did not know about it. Or, he knew about it and thought he could do better on his own, bypassing the middleman. By the unfortunate turn of events he was forced, himself, to become a middleman and sell the shells so that he might pay the freight.

It's exasperating. The man made no effort to find a conveniently located expert who could tell him what to order; the African official did not attempt to find an authority at home who could prevent him from making a fool of himself. Obviously, both believed that there was no such animal as a conchologist, that a shell is a shell is a shell.

Another African official, a trade commissioner in Tanzania, wrote me of his desire for a mutually profitable business relationship. It so happened that I had a marvelous man in Zanzibar, Tanzania, to whom I might have told him to turn for advice. My man, however, was a Hindu; the daily press informed me that the government was bent on Tanzania for the Tanzanians, which meant making things as difficult as possible for the Indian merchants who owned most of the stores.

There had been much to read between the lines in my man's recent correspondence. He had asked me to delay sending him a check for the incoming order until such time as the local currency was stabilized. What most disturbed me was that he had stopped putting his name and address on the outside of his folded aerogram letters, which could only mean that he feared that there was an intercept order on his mail. I could not risk making his situation more difficult than it already was.

I acknowledged receipt of the commissioner's letter, saying that I was already satisfactorily supplied with shells from his area. I meant the general area, of course, eastern Africa, but he took it provincially and shot back a request for the name of my local supplier. I threw that letter in the wastebasket, feeling that the entire exchange was a cloak-and-dagger plot to get me to state in writing that my friend was exporting without a license or some such punishable offense.

They no longer have to worry about him. The last aerogram I received without external identification said that he was returning to India and that his wife and children had already gone on ahead to find and establish a home.

I hope he got away safely. I hope one day to see his name and new address proudly emblazoned on a letter announcing that he is once more in the shell business. There are many wonderful shells in India, and not a single, solitary dealer who can tell one from another. And it's a big country, in need of every cent it can salvage from its national resources.

Something encouraging happened this week. The trade representative of the Philippine Consulate in New York telephoned me, made an appointment, and came to see the shop. I once thought that anyone who grew up in such a paradise of shells as the Philippines would know and love every one of them. I am wiser now so I was not surprised by the gentleman's astonishment at what he saw on my shelves.

SHE SELLS SEASHELLS

As a boy his toys had been Snakeshead and Money Cowries, and he had thought that was all of it, just as a youngster from Long Island envisions a world full of only jingle shells. I showed him twenty or so species from his homeland. The corner of the tent lifted for him and he began to see the possibilities, not of merely shipping out so many billions of bags of cowries per annum but of doing things more intelligently.

Until I told him he had not known that there was a handful of dealers in his islands who were well-informed, who sent out lists, whose bins were frequently too empty to fill the subsequent orders they received. It was also news to him that there are three or four collections in private hands in the Philippines that are the envy of the shell world. He had not known that anyone, of any importance and beyond the age of ten, cared.

It has long been my belief that what the shell business needs is systematic organization. I'm not asking for a Ministry of Conchology with Cabinet rank, but there should be, in every national government, someone who will conscientiously study the subject and absorb enough of it to be able to train a corps of Johnny Appleseeds to spread the word. Every promising local brain should be picked for whatever shred of information it can furnish. Shell collecting should be given the dignity and status it deserves.

As things now stand, the business is a shambles. If all the individuals in the Philippines who write me pathetic letters saying, "Kind Lady, please buy my seashells because my family is poor" had a receptive ear closer at hand into which they could pour their troubles, I would certainly be happier and so would they. Ideally they should have available a local outlet which would buy from them and send me a comprehensive list, instead of all those appeals, from which I could order with reasonable certainty as to what I would get.

The gentleman from the consulate was fired with enthusiasm after we had discussed this. He bought two books, the basic tools of identification, to start the ball rolling. He was particularly pleased that I was also interested in buying land- and tree-snails, which had never seemed of the slightest worth to him. Terrestrial snails from the Philippines, among the world's handsomest, are a produce destroying problem for the plantation owner which he might well turn to profit. Filipinos eat the snails, burning the shell to get the meat out more easily. Hold your fire, boys! Use a pick instead. I'm buying!

I warned the gentleman, Mr. España, not to expect riches overnight since there is an awful lot of homework to be done at this end. Too many people smart enough to tell a hawk from a handsaw still can't tell a cone from a cowry, but many are learning. The future looks bright, if a little distant.

Now and again someone pauses outside my shop, looks in the window, and wonders aloud how a man can possibly make a living selling just seashells. The answer is: he, or in my case she can't. Not yet. Not when so many thousands of people haven't an inkling of the marvelous things she has for sale. The best she can hope for financially is supplementary income. However, although not making a living she can make a wonderful life, enjoying the company of those enthusiasts who have already discovered shells and the unending fascination of her merchandise.

And she can blow a blast on a Triton's Trumpet (*Charonia tritonis*, Linné, from the South Pacific) that may eventually tumble the walls that keep seashells from people.

Bibliography

For the
Well-Dressed
Conchological Bookshelf

A single volume identifying all of the world's seashells would be too heavy to lift. Only a few books on this list even attempt worldwide coverage; the others deal solely with one geographical region or one genus of mollusks.

I have limited myself to books in the English language which are generally available, currently in print, or promised for the near future. There are, of course, books in other languages as well as scientific publications and old books as rare and hard to find as the most elusive seashells.

ABBOTT, R. TUCKER, *American Seashells* (Princeton: D. Van Nostrand); *Caribbean Seashells,* with Germaine Warmke (Narberth, Pa.: Livingston Publishing); *How To Know American Marine Shells* (New York: Signet); *Introducing Seashells* (Princeton: D. Van Nostrand); *Seashells of the World* (Racine, Wisc.: Golden Press); *Van Nos-*

trand's Standard Catalog of Shells, with Robert J. L. Wagner (Princeton: D. Van Nostrand).

ALLAN, JOYCE, *Australian Shells* (Newton Centre, Mass.: Charles T. Branford); *Cowry Shells of World Seas* (Newton Centre, Mass.: Charles T. Branford).

BOUSFIELD, E. L., *Canadian Atlantic Sea Shells* (Ottawa: National Museum of Canada).

BURGESS, C. M., *The Living Cowries* (New York: A. S. Barnes).

CAMERON, RODERICK, *Shells* (New York: G. P. Putnam's Sons).

CERNOHORSKY, W. O., *Marine Shells of the Pacific* (Sydney, Australia: Pacific Publications).

DANCE, S. PETER, *Shell Collecting, an Illustrated History* (Berkeley: University of California Press).

HABE, TADASHIGA, *Shells of the Western Pacific in Color,* Vol. 2 (Osaka, Japan: Hoikusha).

HOYT, MURRAY, *Jewels from the Ocean Deep* (New York: G. P. Putnam's Sons).

JOHNSTONE, K. Y., *Sea Treasure* (Boston: Houghton Mifflin).

KEEN, MYRA, *Sea Shells of Tropical West America* (Stanford: Stanford University Press).

KIRA, TETSUAKI, *Shells of the Western Pacific in Color,* Vol. 1 (Osaka, Japan: Hoikusha).

MARSH, J. A., and RIPPINGALE, O. H., *Cone Shells of the World* (Brisbane, Australia: Jacaranda Press).

MELVIN, A. GORDON, *Sea Shells of the World with Values* (Rutland, Vt., and Tokyo: Charles E. Tuttle).

MORRIS, PERCY A., *A Field Guide to the Shells of Our Atlantic and Gulf Coasts* (Boston: Houghton Mifflin); *A Field Guide to Shells of the Pacific Coast and Hawaii* (Boston: Houghton Mifflin).

ROGERS, JULIA E., *The Shell Book* (Newton Centre, Mass.: Charles T. Branford).

TRAVERS, LOUISE A., *The Romance of Shells in Nature and Art* (New York: M. Barrows and Company).

WEBB, WALTER M., *Foreign Land Shells* (Wellesley Hills, Mass.: Lee Publications); *Handbook for Shell Collectors* (Wellesley Hills, Mass.: Lee Publications).

Index

INDEX

INDEX